CAMPAIGN 385

STALINGRAD 1942–43 (3)

Catastrophe: the Death of 6th Army

ROBERT FORCZYK

ILLUSTRATED BY STEVE NOON
Series editor Nikolai Bogdanovic

OSPREY PUBLISHING
Bloomsbury Publishing Plc
Kemp House, Chawley Park, Cumnor Hill, Oxford OX2 9PH, UK
29 Earlsfort Terrace, Dublin 2, Ireland
1385 Broadway, 5th Floor, New York, NY 10018, USA
E-mail: info@ospreypublishing.com
www.ospreypublishing.com

OSPREY is a trademark of Osprey Publishing Ltd

First published in Great Britain in 2022

A catalogue record for this book is available from the British Library.

ISBN: PB 9781472842732; eBook 9781472842749; ePDF 9781472842718;
XML 9781472842725

22 23 24 25 26   10 9 8 7 6 5 4 3 2 1

Maps by Bounford.com
3D BEVs by Paul Kime
Index by Janet Andrew
Typeset by PDQ Digital Media Solutions, Bungay, UK
Printed and bound in India by Replika Press Private Ltd.

MIX
Paper from
responsible sources
FSC® C016779
www.fsc.org

Artist's note

Readers may care to note that the original paintings from which the colour
plates in this book were prepared are available for private sale. All
reproduction copyright whatsoever is retained by the publishers. The artist
can be contacted via the website below:

www.steve-noon.co.uk

The publishers regret that they can enter into no correspondence upon
this matter.

Osprey Publishing supports the Woodland Trust, the UK's leading woodland
conservation charity.

To find out more about our authors and books visit
www.ospreypublishing.com. Here you will find extracts, author
interviews, details of forthcoming events and the option to sign up for
our newsletter.

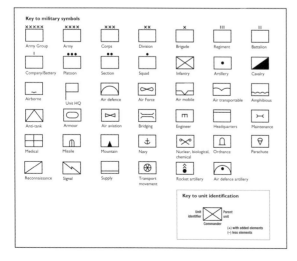

Front cover main image: German troops retreat into Stalingrad,
2100hrs, 22 January 1943. (Steve Noon)

Title page image: German troops move cautiously past the wreck
of a knocked-out T-34 tank. (Nik Cornish at www.Stavka.org.uk)

CONTENTS

ORIGINS OF THE CAMPAIGN   4

CHRONOLOGY   6

OPPOSING COMMANDERS   7
Soviet . Axis

OPPOSING FORCES   12
Soviet . Axis . Orders of Battle, 19 November 1942

OPPOSING PLANS   20
Soviet . Axis

THE CAMPAIGN   27
Operation *Uranus*, 19–23 November 1942 . The initial German reaction, 24–28 November 1942
The Battle of the Chir River, 30 November–15 December 1942 . *Wintergewitter*, 12–29 December 1942
Little Saturn, 16–28 December 1942 . Stalingrad *Kesselschlacht*, 1–31 December 1942
Operation *Ring* and the end of 6.Armee, 1 January–2 February 1943

ANALYSIS   88

THE BATTLEFIELD TODAY   92

FURTHER READING   94

INDEX   95

ORIGINS OF THE CAMPAIGN

After failing to destroy the Red Army with Operation *Barbarossa*, the invasion of the Soviet Union in 1941, Adolf Hitler decided to make a second attempt to achieve a decisive victory over his nemesis in the summer of 1942. No longer strong enough to mount attacks in all sectors, the German *Ostheer* (Army in the East) instead focused its efforts in southern Russia. Operation *Blau* (*Blue*) envisioned advances by two German army groups: Heeresgruppe B towards Stalingrad on the Volga River, and Heeresgruppe A moving to occupy the Soviet oilfields in the Caucasus. Beginning in late June 1942, Operation *Blau* initially achieved success, seizing the cities of Rostov and Voronezh. Yet instead of standing fast and becoming encircled by fast-moving German panzer spearheads, Stalin authorized the Soviet armies in the south to conduct tactical withdrawals in order to avoid annihilation. Soviet resistance did stiffen as Heeresgruppe B approached the Don and its advance units did not reach the Volga until late August. Soviet forces in the Stalingrad sector were badly battered after heavy fighting, and for a short time it looked as though the city might fall at any moment.

However, Stalin ordered that the city would be held at all costs, and the Red Army employed draconian measures to instill the will to fight. Chuikov's defending 62nd Army was ordered to hold or die. Shirkers and deserters were executed. On the other side, Paulus' 6.Armee had already suffered about 40,000 casualties in the nine-week advance to reach Stalingrad, but began moving into the city in mid-September. The Luftwaffe dominated the skies over Stalingrad and provided powerful fire support that made up for the shortage of infantry on the ground. The result was a two-month-long slug-fest between an irresistible force and an immovable object, which resulted in heavy casualties on both sides, reducing the city to burning, shattered rubble. Between 13 September and 11 November, 6.Armee conducted five major attacks in Stalingrad, which succeeded in overrunning a number of key industrial facilities, such as the Stalingrad Tractor Factory (STZ) and the Barrikady Factory. Chuikov's 62nd Army suffered about 100,000 casualties in two months, but managed to retain control over parts of central Stalingrad. Ultimately, 6.Armee ran out of infantry before it could accomplish its mission. By mid-November, Paulus' 6.Armee had lost much of its combat effectiveness, with over 20,000 dead and wounded just in the city fighting. Not only was 6.Armee left in a debilitated condition, but Heeresgruppe B had been forced to draw German units from the vulnerable flanks, in order to keep the offensive at Stalingrad going. By early November, 6.Armee's left flank along the Don was protected by Romanian and Italian troops, while its

The protracted defence of Stalingrad by Chuikov's 62nd Army set the stage for the Red Army's eventual victory in the campaign. By mid-November 1942, 6.Armee was over-extended, poorly supplied and its flanks were protected by poorly equipped Romanian troops. It was a recipe for disaster. (Author's collection)

right flank was held by a mixed German–Romanian force. Unsurprisingly, the leadership of Heeresgruppe B was nervous about the arrival of winter weather, which increased the risk of Soviet attacks on these vulnerable flanks.

During the fighting inside Stalingrad, the Stalingrad Front had conducted one counter-offensive after another against 6.Armee's left flank, primarily in the Kotluban sector, which all failed. Although these attacks did divert some German resources away from the city fighting, the German forces in this sector were too well entrenched to be driven out. Limited attacks south of Stalingrad, from the Beketovka salient, had also failed to achieve much success. As a result, the Red Army squandered a significant amount of manpower and equipment, but gradually recognized that solid German defensive lines could not be broken under conditions (lack of surprise, enemy air superiority) that favoured the enemy. While the Red Army had not been defeated at Stalingrad, by November 1942 the leadership finally accepted that a different approach was needed in order to achieve victory.

This is the third volume in a trilogy that covers the entire Stalingrad campaign from June 1942 until February 1943. Volume 1 covered Operation *Blau* and the German advance to the Volga, the period from 28 June to 1 September 1942. Volume 2 covered the fighting in and around Stalingrad from September to November 1942, and this third volume covers the Soviet counter-offensive, from November 1942 to February 1943. Operations in the Caucasus, already covered in Osprey Campaign No. 28: *The Caucasus 1942–43: Kleist's Race for Oil*, are only discussed in passing in this trilogy.

The 6.Armee's infantry units were badly worn down after three months of intense urban combat and its infantry battalions were often reduced to company-size detachments. Paulus had difficulty holding his front lines even before the Soviet counter-offensive, and the bulk of his remaining combat power was located near Stalingrad, with little left in reserve. (Author's collection)

CHRONOLOGY

1942

6 October Eremenko proposes a new plan for a counter-offensive at Stalingrad.

13 October Stalin approves the draft plan for the new counter-offensive.

22 October Stavka authorizes the re-creation of the South-Western Front.

4 November Stavka finalizes the plans for Operation *Uranus*.

19 November Operation *Uranus* begins: South-Western Front and Don Front attack the Romanian Third Army.

20 November Soviet 51st and 57th armies attack Romanian forces near Lake Sarpa.

Hitler orders the creation of Heeresgruppe Don.

22 November Kalach is captured by the 26th Tank Corps.

23 November The Soviets complete the encirclement of the Stalingrad pocket.

24 November Hitler orders Paulus to hold on and await relief.

The Luftwaffe begins the Stalingrad airlift.

7 December The 5th Tank Army launches a major attack against Gruppe Hollidt on the Chir River.

12 December Operation *Wintergewitter* (*Winter Storm*) begins.

13 December The 5th Shock Army attacks on the Chir River.

16 December Operation *Little Saturn* begins: Voronezh and South-Western fronts attack the Italian Eighth Army.

19 December Manstein issues 'Thunderclap' codeword to 6.Armee, ordering a breakout, but Paulus refuses.

24 December Tatsinskaya airfield is captured by the Soviet 24th Tank Corps.

The Stalingrad Front begins the Kotelnikovo offensive.

29 December The Supreme High Command of the German Army (Oberkommando des Heeres, OKH) authorizes Heeresgruppe A to withdraw from the Caucasus.

Kotelnikovo is captured by the Soviet 2nd Guards Army.

1943

2 January Morozovsk airfield is captured by the 3rd Guards Army.

10 January Operation *Ring* begins: the Don Front attacks 6.Armee.

13 January Voronezh Front begins its offensive against the Hungarian 2nd Army.

16 January Pitomnik airfield is lost.

23 January Gumrak airfield is lost.

26 January The 6.Armee is split into two pockets.

31 January Paulus surrenders.

2 February The northern pocket in Stalingrad surrenders.

OPPOSING COMMANDERS

SOVIET

The Soviet command structure for Operation *Uranus* was complicated, since it involved the coordination of three different fronts. General objectives were defined by the State Defence Committee (*Gosudarstvennyj Komitet Oborony*, GKO) and Stavka in Moscow, but operations were conducted by front- and army-level staffs. Up to this point in the war, multi-front operations had not been a strong suit for the Red Army, so Stavka developed a system of using representatives to oversee operational planning in subordinate formations. Zhukov and Vasilevskiy were the two most important Stavka representatives involved with *Uranus*, but other senior command cadres were sent to help plan

General-leytenant Nikolai F. Vatutin, commander of the South-Western Front. The 41-year-old Vatutin was one of the rising stars in the Red Army, and he was chosen to lead the main effort in Operation *Uranus*. (Author's collection)

artillery fire support and air operations. Front-level political commissars, such as Nikita S. Khrushchev, also influenced operational-level decision-making. However, the Red Army was fortunate in that it had three of its very best operational-level commanders in key command positions for *Uranus*, and for once these men were granted the latitude to conduct a professional style of warfare.

General-leytenant Nikolai F. Vatutin (1901–44) was made commander of the South-Western Front on 25 October 1942. Born into a peasant family from Voronezh, Vatutin had an amazing and unusual career. After being drafted into the Red Army in 1920, he rose quickly from enlisted soldier to the officer ranks and graduated from the General Staff Academy in 1937. By 1940, Vatutin was chief of operations in the Soviet General Staff. At the start of the Russo-German War, Vatutin was sent to Leningrad to serve as chief of staff of the North-Western Front, where he organized successful counter-attacks at Soltsy and Staraya Russa that delayed the German advance. During the Winter Counter-Offensive, Vatutin planned the encirclement of German forces at Demyansk, although the enemy ultimately relieved the pocket. In July 1942, Vatutin was sent to command the Voronezh Front, and

General-polkovnik Konstantin K. Rokossovsky, commander of the Don Front. Although Rokossovsky only played a supporting role in Operation *Uranus*, he was given primary responsibility for crushing the encircled 6.Armee. He proved capable in orchestrating complex, multi-army attacks around the pocket. (Author's collection)

was obliged to mount several counter-attacks to try to retake the city – which failed. Nevertheless, he was selected to command the main effort for Operation *Uranus*, based in part on Zhukov's recommendation. At 41, Vatutin lacked the command experience of the German commanders and even many of his Soviet peers, but he was intelligent, aggressive and had a head for operational-level warfare. The selection of Vatutin to lead the South-Western Front in *Uranus* was one of the more inspired Soviet leadership decisions made during the war.

General-polkovnik Konstantin K. Rokossovsky (1896–1968) was commander of the Don Front. Rokossovsky was of mixed Polish–Belarusian lineage, and during World War I he served as an enlisted cavalryman in the Tsarist Army. He joined the Red Army in 1917 and saw considerable action in the Russian Civil War, rising to command a cavalry regiment. During the interwar period, Rokossovsky served with both Eremenko and Zhukov, and was given command of a cavalry corps by 1936. However, Rokossovsky was one of the victims of the Stalinist purges. He was arrested by the NKVD and spent over two years in prison; during this time, he was severely beaten and had most of his front teeth knocked out. In March 1940, Rokossovsky was released and rehabilitated, in part due to his cavalry connections. He was given command of the newly formed 9th Mechanized Corps, which he led in the Battle of Dubno in June 1941. After the initial border battles, Rokossovsky was sent to the Western Front, where he commanded the 16th Army during the defence of Moscow. Rokossovsky's army was decimated in heavy fighting, but he blocked the German advance to Moscow. In March 1942, Rokossovsky was badly wounded by artillery shellfire and he was sidelined for two months. During the initial stages of *Blau*, Rokossovsky's 16th Army conducted an unsuccessful counter-offensive against the German 2.Panzer-Armee north of Bryansk; although a failure, the operation taught Rokossovsky quite a bit about German defensive tactics. After a brief stint as commander of the Bryansk Front, Rokossovsky was selected to command the new Don Front. By November 1942, Rokossovsky was a veteran front commander who had gained valuable experience in handling armour, infantry and artillery in complex operations.

General-polkovnik Andrei I. Eremenko (1892–1970) took command of the South-East Front on 7 August, then the Stalingrad Front on 23 August. Eremenko came from a peasant background and served as a non-commissioned officer in the Imperial Russian Army from 1914 to 1917. During the Russian Civil War, Eremenko began his career as a cavalry officer in the *Konarmia* (Cavalry Army), and during the interwar period he commanded first a regiment, then a division. In 1939, Eremenko commanded the 6th Cavalry Corps in the invasion of Poland. Afterwards, Eremenko was transferred to the Far East, but was hurriedly brought back to Moscow in response to the German invasion. Taking command of the hard-pressed Western Front, Eremenko briefly stalled the German advance at Smolensk, but was wounded. Transferred to command of the newly raised Bryansk Front, Eremenko's command was shattered in the opening days of Operation *Typhoon* and he was again wounded. Despite his wounds, Eremenko was given command of the 4th Shock Army during the Winter Counter-Offensive and he succeeded in liberating Toropets. However, Eremenko was wounded a third time in January 1942, and he spent the next six months recovering. Eremenko had served as the primary Soviet operational-level commander during the first three months of the Battle of Stalingrad, and by November 1942 he was thoroughly familiar with the enemy, terrain and weather in this sector.

General-polkovnik Andrei I. Eremenko, commander of the Stalingrad Front. Eremenko was one of the key Soviet leaders throughout the Stalingrad campaign, playing a major role in both the defensive phase and the counter-offensive. (Author's collection)

General-leytenant Prokofiy L. Romanenko (1897–1949) had commanded the 5th Tank Army since 1 November 1942. Romanenko came from a Ukrainian peasant family and served as a cavalry non-commissioned officer in the Tsarist Army during World War I. Joining the Red Army in 1918, Romanenko commanded a cavalry regiment in the *Konarmia* and fought in the Battle of Tsaritsyn (the former name of Stalingrad). He served as a military advisor during the Spanish Civil War in 1937 and switched to mechanized forces. In 1940, Romanenko commanded the 8th Mechanized Corps in the Russo-Finnish War, but the performance of Soviet armour was unsatisfactory. Although Romanenko remained an advocate for creating strong mechanized shock groups, he found himself sent to the Trans-Baikal district and thus missed the initial stages of the German invasion in 1941. Romanenko was not brought back to Moscow until early 1942, where he was tasked with organizing and leading the 3rd Tank Army. Zhukov decided to employ the 3rd Tank Army in an ill-judged counter-offensive north of Orel in late August, which proved to be a disaster. Romanenko lost two-thirds of his armour for negligible gain, and in the process learned painful lessons about logistics and command and control in mechanized operations. Romanenko was a capable commander, but the Red Army's armoured forces were still evolving and made plenty of mistakes, for which he was often blamed.

AXIS

Generaloberst Maximilian von Weichs (1881–1954) had been commander of Heeresgruppe B since July 1942. As army group commander, von Weichs had to be concerned about a front that extended from Voronezh all the way

ABOVE LEFT
General der Panzertruppe Friedrich Paulus, commander of 6.Armee. Paulus proved to be an uninspired choice to lead the Wehrmacht's main effort in 1942. Prior to Operation *Uranus*, Paulus had demonstrated little initiative in developing contingency measures to protect his flanks. Once his army was encircled, Paulus proved incapable of deciding to breakout. (Courtesy of the Central Museum of the Armed Forces, Moscow via Stavka)

ABOVE RIGHT
Generaloberst Hermann Hoth, commander of 4.Panzer-Armee at the start of Operation *Uranus*. Although unable to protect Paulus' right flank with his diminished forces, he managed to organize a relief effort that gave Eremenko considerable distress throughout December 1942. Hoth was one of Germany's premier Panzer leaders at this point in the war, but even he could not save 6.Armee. (Author's collection)

out to the Volga, as well as dealing with subordinate Hungarian, Italian and Romanian armies. Once it became obvious that 6.Armee could not complete the conquest of Stalingrad prior to the onset of winter weather, von Weichs became increasingly apprehensive about the threat of a Soviet counter-offensive against his army group's extended front along the Don. However, von Weichs was an elderly aristocrat and lacked the stomach for the kind of heated arguments with Hitler and the OKH required to extract additional reinforcements. Ignoring von Weichs' feeble requests, the OKH instead sent the limited amount of reserves available to support Heeresgruppe Mitte's defence of the Rzhev salient. While adequate as a senior commander when operations were proceeding well, von Weichs lacked the *Fingerspitzengefühl* (situational awareness) required to handle a fast-moving crisis and Hitler soon recognized his limitations.

General der Panzertruppe Friedrich Paulus (1890–1957) had commanded 6.Armee since January 1942. Paulus had made his reputation in the Heer as a diligent, hard-working staff officer, not as a field commander. During the advance to Stalingrad and subsequent three-month-long battle for the city, Paulus proved to be a methodical, set-piece tactician. To his credit, Paulus recognized early on that his army lacked the resources to complete its mission and that the Red Army posed a significant threat to his flanks, but contented himself with whining to von Weichs. Paulus did not deploy his available panzers to serve as a mobile reserve to defeat an enemy counter-offensive and should have ensured that key positions such as Kalach were fortified. Once his army was isolated, Paulus demonstrated little concern for his starving soldiers and proved unwilling to disobey Hitler and make the hard choices needed to save at least some of his troops. Paulus also allowed his chief of staff, Generalmajor Arthur Schmidt, to take over many of his command responsibilities, thereby reducing himself to an ineffectual cipher. In a crisis, Paulus became a weak, vacillating, self-concerned commander, which is the antithesis of military leadership.

Generaloberst Hermann Hoth (1885–1971) took command of 4.Panzer-Armee on 15 May 1942. Hoth was a Prussian infantryman and General Staff-trained officer who rose steadily through the ranks of the Wehrmacht in the 1930s. During the Polish and French campaigns, he ably led XV.Armee-Korps (mot.), then Panzergruppe 3 during *Barbarossa* in 1941. Hoth managed to avoid being sacked by Hitler during the winter battles and was given command of 17.Armee, helping to stabilize the southern front after the loss of Rostov. By 1942, Hoth was one of the most experienced and aggressive German operational-level manoeuvre commanders and he knew how to get the best out of his *Panzer-Divisionen*. Indeed, Hoth demonstrated great operational command skill during the opening weeks of *Blau*, marking him

as one of the best German manoeuvre commanders of World War II. He also knew how to work well with other commanders and to avoid trying to debate directives from Hitler. Once 6.Armee was surrounded at Stalingrad, Hoth was the logical choice to lead the relief effort.

General de armată Petre I. Dumitrescu (1882–1950) had commanded the Romanian Third Army since March 1941. Dumitrescu was commissioned as an artillery officer in the Romanian Army in 1903 and commanded an artillery battery in World War I. During the Interwar Period, Dumitrescu spent seven years as chief of operations in the Romanian General Staff and two years as a military attaché in Paris. He was then given command of an infantry division in 1933, a corps in 1937 and an army in 1940. Dumitrescu commanded the Romanian Third Army during Operation *Barbarossa* in 1941, supporting the advance of the German 11.Armee to the Crimea. During the initial stages of *Blau*, Dumitrescu's Third Army accompanied Heeresgruppe A into the Caucasus and successfully cleared Soviet forces out of the Kuban. Afterwards, Third Army was shifted to support Heeresgruppe B's defence along the Don River in early October. Dumitrescu recognized that this was a dangerously vulnerable sector and recommended that the Soviet bridgeheads over the Don should be eliminated, but he was ignored by von Weichs. Dumitrescu was a competent commander, although something of a ticket-puncher, who could accomplish his missions when properly resourced.

General Petre Dumitrescu, commander of the Romanian Third Army. Dumitrescu was a competent commander, but was not provided the resources to accomplish his mission of protecting the extended left flank of 6.Armee. Despite the destruction of his army, Dumitrescu was given another command in the Ukraine, and remained in the field until Romania switched sides in August 1944. (Author's collection)

OPPOSING FORCES

SOVIET

Altogether, the three Soviet fronts involved in Operation *Uranus* comprised just over 1 million troops in ten armies. These three fronts had roughly one-sixth of the Red Army's total field strength, with 66 rifle divisions, six cavalry divisions, five tank army corps and two mechanized corps. Overall, the Red Army enjoyed a 2:1 numerical superiority or better in the Stalingrad sector and Stavka still had ample reserves to support follow-on operations.

Infantry
The Soviet rifle divisions on the South-Western Front were in the best condition, since many had recently arrived from the *Rezerv Verkhovnogo Glavnokomandovaniya* (RVGK) reserves, with an average strength of 8,800 men (84 per cent of the strength authorized by the July 1942 divisional *Shtat*). In contrast, the battle-worn rifle divisions on the Don and Stalingrad fronts were typically around 50–55 per cent of their authorized strengths. In terms of organic artillery support, the Soviet 1942 rifle division was supposed to have 32 76mm field guns and 12 122mm howitzers, as well as 18 120mm mortars. Romanenko's 5th Tank Army was provided with six rifle divisions for the breakthrough battle, including three veteran guards rifle divisions. Soviet rifle divisions were more than a match for Romanian infantry divisions, although they still struggled to reduce positions defended by German troops. Once the mobile phase of *Uranus* began, only motorized rifle troops were able to keep up with the fast-moving mechanized units, leaving the 'leg' rifle units to mop-up scattered enemy pockets. Soviet commanders ordered tank units to carry some infantrymen on each vehicle, enabling some troops to keep up with the advance. Otherwise, over snow-covered terrain the bulk of Soviet infantry could only advance slowly. The Red Army's rifle troops would also bear the brunt of the fighting to reduce the Stalingrad pocket, once *Uranus* succeeded in encircling 6.Armee.

Armour
Despite the fact that Soviet industry produced over 24,000 tanks in 1942, the Red Army had difficulty filling out and replenishing its battle-weary armoured units. The T-34/76 Model 1942 medium tank was the best Soviet tank, optimized for long-distance movement over open terrain, but there were never enough of them. Consequently, nearly half the armour in Soviet tank

The Red Army's trump card in the final phase of the Stalingrad campaign was armour, which it was finally able to mass in the right place and at the right time to achieve decisive results. The T-34/76 Model 1943 tank possessed excellent mobility and firepower, enabling it to move long distances over snow and ice. However, the horse team in the foreground demonstrates an important point – that the Red Army of 1942 was still heavily dependent upon horses to move supplies across the winter steppe. (Author's collection)

brigades consisted of T-60 and T-70 light tanks, which lacked the firepower and armoured protection of the T-34. Most of the KV-1 heavy tanks were massed in separate breakthrough tank regiments, including three provided to the 21st Army. The two cavalry corps were also provided tank support to enhance their firepower, including some KV-8 flamethrower tanks. During *Uranus*, the Red Army employed a total of 1,550 tanks, including 239 KV-1s, 712 T-34s and 599 light tanks.

Each of the five tank corps involved in *Uranus* had 135–150 tanks, but these formations were still handicapped by limited organic infantry and artillery support. Consequently, the tank corps had little ability to seize fortified towns and even less to hold captured terrain. The GKO recognized the organizational shortcomings of the tank corps and had begun to form several new mechanized corps in September 1942; the 4th Mechanized Corps was assigned to the Stalingrad Front for *Uranus*. Enormous resources were poured into forming the 4th Mechanized Corps, which not only had 179 tanks, but nine motorized rifle battalions (6,000 infantry), 100 armoured cars and 2,000 trucks. In Operation *Uranus*, Soviet armoured units were optimized to conduct a Deep Battle-style operation, in order to disrupt the enemy front and then push deep into their rear areas – a type of operation the Red Army had not yet successfully accomplished.

Artillery support

Operation *Uranus* enjoyed considerably more artillery support than previous Red Army offensives, and Soviet-era accounts claim that over 22,000 artillery pieces and mortars of all calibres were committed to support the offensive. In fact, the actual number of medium- and heavy-calibre guns was about 2,000. Yet these numbers alone provide little insight into the Red Army's improved ability to employ its indirect fire assets. Stavka had just begun to form artillery divisions to provide concentrated fire support for breakthrough battles, and both the Don Front and South-Western fronts received one artillery division, each of which controlled up to 12 regiments with over 200 guns, howitzers and heavy mortars. However, an artillery division at this point still relied heavily on short-range 76mm field guns and 120mm mortars, while typically only possessing 36 152mm howitzers. Altogether, Stavka provided 39 artillery regiments and 33 Guards mortar regiments (BM-13) from the RVGK reserves.

The Red Army was also learning to use its artillery differently. General-polkovnik Nikolai N. Voronov, commander-in-chief of the Red Army's artillery and a Stavka representative, closely supervised the development of the artillery fire support plans for Operation *Uranus*. Most of the RVGK heavy mortars and multiple rocket launchers would be massed to provide short-range support fires for the infantry assault groups, while the heavy 152mm howitzers would be massed into long-range groups to strike targets in the depth of the enemy defences. At this point, the Red Army's artillery had negligible ability to conduct counter-battery fire against Axis artillery units and favoured tightly scripted artillery plans. Artillery forward observers were capable of directing fire onto point targets, but Soviet artillery barrages tended to favour area-wide suppression over engaging specific aim points. Furthermore, the Red Army's artillery had limited ability to support a fast-moving offensive and required time to move forward to new positions. Consequently, the Red Army's artillery arm of late 1942 was capable of massive – although not particularly accurate or responsive – fire support.

Air support
The Soviet Voyenno-Vozdushnye Sily (VVS, Army Air Forces) hoped to support Operation *Uranus* with air support from four air armies (2nd, 8th, 16th and 17th Vozdushnaya Armiya, VA), which possessed a total of over 1,100 operational aircraft, although winter weather limited the number of combat sorties to only about 200 per day in late November. In the Stalingrad sector, the VVS could deploy 380 operational fighters, mostly Yak-1s, against about 50 German Bf 109G and 30 Romanian IAR 80 fighters. For the first time, the VVS would be able to commit over 400 Il-2 Sturmoviks to an operation, which was expected to boost close air support provided to the army. However, the four air armies only had 140 operational daylight bombers (Pe-2 and Boston), mostly in the 17th VA, which limited their ability to strike enemy airfields and railway stations behind the lines. Once Stalingrad was surrounded, the VVS was tasked with disrupting the German airlift to the besieged 6.Armee, which would prove difficult given the lack of radar warning and poor visibility around the city.

AXIS

In mid-November 1942, Heeresgruppe B had about 457,000 troops operating in the Stalingrad sector, of whom slightly more than half were Romanian. The German 6.Armee and rump 4.Panzer-Armee had a total of 21 divisions, while the Romanian Third Army and forming Fourth Army had 18 divisions. Due to personnel shortages, 6.Armee employed about 58,000 former Soviet soldiers (known as *Hilfswillige* or Hiwis, these prisoners volunteered to serve) as labour and support troops. The 6.Armee started its final battle desperately short of front-line personnel, and those who remained were exhausted, since the OKH had not provided any significant reinforcements to this sector since the Battle of Stalingrad had begun in September.

Romanian

The Romanian Third Army consisted of 11 divisions (eight infantry, two cavalry and one armoured) with a total of 155,492 troops. The Romanian Fourth Army – which was still forming in the 4.Panzer-Armee area but not yet activated – had about 75,000 troops in seven divisions (five infantry and two cavalry). One additional Romanian infantry division served in the German IV.Armee-Korps. The Romanian Army had already suffered heavy losses in Russia since June 1941, and by November 1942 most infantry divisions in the Stalingrad sector possessed about 70 per cent of their authorized personnel strength. As a result, Romanian infantry divisions were reduced from nine to six infantry battalions. Romanian infantry units were particularly weak in terms of anti-tank and artillery firepower; their obsolescent 37mm and 47mm anti-tank guns were ineffective against the Soviet T-34 and KV-1 tanks. Each infantry division had just 24 75mm guns and 24 100mm howitzers, which was further aggravated by the shortage of artillery ammunition. In addition, the Romanian Third Army had 80 heavy field howitzers and the nascent Fourth Army was assigned 60 heavy howitzers; these were a mix of modern Škoda-built weapons and old French pieces. On the positive side, the Romanians had managed to construct adequate field works, which protected them from enemy artillery fire, and to emplace barbed-wire obstacles and mines to hinder enemy armour.

Romanian infantry in early November 1942, prior to the start of Operation *Uranus*. The Romanian troops were required to defend very long sectors along the Don River, but without the benefit of adequate artillery or anti-tank weaponry. Nevertheless, many Romanian units displayed admirable fighting spirit when struck by some of the best units in the Red Army. (Süddeutsche Zeitung, Bild 00384722, Foto: Scherl)

Not only were the Romanians forced to hold dangerously wide sectors, but they also had little in the way of tactical reserves. The best force available, the Romanian 1st Armoured Division, had two armoured battalions (equipped with the Czech-made R-2 light tank), four motorized infantry battalions, three motorized artillery battalions, as well as motorized anti-tank, engineer and reconnaissance battalions. On paper, the 1st Armoured Division looked like a well-rounded combined-arms team, but the obsolescence of most of its equipment greatly reduced its actual capabilities. In particular, the R-2 light tank was hopelessly outclassed on the battlefield of 1942 and could not go head-to-head with Soviet armour. A few weeks prior to *Uranus*, the Germans provided 20 medium tanks (Panzer III Ausf. N and Panzer IV Ausf. G) to try to reinforce the Romanian 1st Armoured Division, but the Romanian crews had just begun training on the new vehicles. In addition, the Romanians tried to use their cavalry divisions as tactical reserves, although these brigade-size formations had very few trucks or horses for mobility and usually ended up fighting as foot infantry.

German infantry

Due to the inability to fully replace losses, German infantry divisions were in a state of flux in late 1942, with most divisions having six to eight infantry battalions. Although there was no standard organization by this point in the war, authorized strength was supposed to be around 15,000 men. In 6.Armee, most infantry divisions had around 7,000–10,000 troops, with the average ration strength (*Verpflegungsstärke*) being 8,676 (57 per cent of authorized strength).

The Romanian 1st Armoured Division had 84 operational R-2 lights tanks at the start of Operation *Uranus*. The R-2 was the Skoda-built LT V2 35, armed with a 37mm gun. By the standards of late 1942, the R-2 was hopelessly obsolete and lacked the firepower or mobility to stand up to the latest Soviet tanks. (Süddeutsche Zeitung, Bild 01126285)

Combat strengths (*Kampfstärke*) were much less, averaging just 3,000–5,000 men per division. The strongest infantry division in 6.Armee – 44.Infanterie-Division in XI.Armee-Korps – had not been involved in any fighting in the city. The weakness of the German infantry extended all the way down to the battalion and company level. Of the 86 infantry battalions in 6.Armee, only 16 were still rated 'strong' or 'medium strong', while 35 were rated 'weak' or 'exhausted'. Some infantry battalions were reduced to less than the strength of one nominal company, and infantry companies often had just 50 troops in the line. Furthermore, the infantry in 6.Armee had been on reduced rations for months, since priority of supply had gone to ammunition, and poor field hygiene led to outbreaks of typhus. The 6.Armee quartermasters had just begun issuing winter clothing when Operation *Uranus* began, so only a few units had received their allocation. The German Panzergrenadiers in the *Panzer-Divisionen* (totaling ten battalions) tended to be in better shape, since these units had higher priority for replacements and supplies.

German armour

The Germans had just over 400 operational tanks and assault guns in the Stalingrad sector in mid-November 1942, but their control was spread across multiple command jurisdictions. Paulus controlled the largest pool of armour, with three *Panzer-Divisionen* (14., 16. and 24.) and two motorized infantry divisions (3. and 60.); altogether, these formations had 218 operational tanks and 36 StuG III assault guns. Hoth's 4.Panzer-Armee controlled two motorized infantry divisions (16. and 29.) with a total of 102 tanks and seven assault guns. Finally, Heeresgruppe B controlled 22.Panzer-Division, which possessed 40 operational tanks. The German Panzer IV Ausf. G armed with the long KwK L/40 cannon (80 available) and the Panzer III Ausf. L armed with the long KwK L/60 cannon (158 available) were both capable of defeating the Soviet T-34 tanks, although their mobility over snow and ice was somewhat inferior. In theory, the Germans had enough armour in the Stalingrad area to prevent *Uranus* from achieving a decisive success, but the best panzers were not massed into a mobile reserve under a single commander and the shortage of fuel limited mobility. Again, the priority of ammunition to sustain the fight in Stalingrad through mid-November meant limited fuel reserves were available east of the Don for Paulus' and Hoth's tanks.

Luftwaffe

After months of heavy combat over Stalingrad, VIII.Fliegerkorps was at a low ebb by mid-November 1942. Some units had been transferred to other theatres or sent to be rebuilt in Germany, leaving just 330 combat aircraft to support the Stalingrad sector. Only 58 per cent of these aircraft were operational when *Uranus* began. Jagdgeschwader 3 had two *Jagdgruppen* equipped with about 50 Bf 109F/G fighters forward-deployed at Pitomnik to provide air cover over 6.Armee. Heeresgruppe B was counting on VIII. Fliegerkorps to strike hard against any Soviet counter-offensive, but the only units available were 13 He 111H bombers from Kampfgeschwader 27 based at Millerovo, 42 Ju 87 Stukas from Sturzkampfgeschwader 2 and 45 fighter-bombers from Schlachtgeschwader 1. Although VIII.Fliegerkorps strike assets were limited in number, they did possess a cadre of skilled veteran pilots, such as Oberleutnant Hans Ulrich Rudel in I./Sturzkampfgeschwader 2. In addition to the Luftwaffe, the Romanian Air Force also provided a large contingent, the Gruparea Aeriană de Luptă (GAL), with over 150 aircraft to support its field armies. Although the Romanian fighter groups, equipped with the Bf 109E and IAR 80A fighters, provided good service, the bomber and reconnaissance units, equipped with a heterogeneous collection of British, French, Italian, German and Polish aircraft, suffered from low serviceability rates.

Another factor of note was the Axis air transport capability in the Don region. Only 25 of the 76 Ju 52 transports in Luftflotte 4 were operational at the start of *Uranus*, along with a small number of Romanian Ju 52 transports. Given that a Ju 52 could carry a nominal cargo load of two tons, Luftflotte 4 had the ability to move about 50 tons of supplies by air per day, given good flying weather. However, the winter weather around Stalingrad – which offered only eight hours of daylight at best – severely hampered flight operations between November 1942 and January 1943, which had a major impact on the Luftwaffe's ability to influence the final stages of the campaign.

ORDERS OF BATTLE, 19 NOVEMBER 1942

SOVIET

SOUTH-WESTERN FRONT (GENERAL-LEYTENANT NIKOLAI F. VATUTIN)

1st Guards Army (General-leytenant Dmitri D. Leliushenko)
1st Rifle Division
153rd Rifle Division
197th Rifle Division
203rd Rifle Division
266th Rifle Division
278th Rifle Division
1st Guards Mechanized Corps (General-major Ivan N. Russianov)
22nd Separate Motorized Rifle Brigade
5th Tank Army (General-leytenant Prokofiy L. Romanenko)
14th Guards Rifle Division
47th Guards Rifle Division
50th Guards Rifle Division
119th Rifle Division
159th Rifle Division
346th Rifle Division
1st Tank Corps (General-major Vasily V. Butkov)
26th Tank Corps (General-major Aleksei G. Rodin)
8th Cavalry Corps (General-major Mikhail D. Borisov)
8th Guards Tank Brigade

21st Army (General-major Ivan M. Chistiakov)
63rd Rifle Division
76th Rifle Division
96th Rifle Division
277th Rifle Division
293rd Rifle Division
333rd Rifle Division
4th Tank Corps (General-major Andrei G. Kravchenko)
3rd Guards Cavalry Corps (General-major Issa A. Pliev)
1st Guards Tank Regiment (separate)
2nd Guards Tank Regiment (separate)
4th Guards Tank Regiment (separate)
1st Artillery Division
2nd Air Army (General-major Konstantin N. Smirnov)
205th Fighter Division
207th Fighter Division
227th Assault Aviation Division
208th Night Bomber Aviation Division
Total operational aircraft: 139, comprising about 30 fighters, 30 Il-2s and 80 U-2s.
17th Air Army (General-major Stepan A. Krasovsky)
1st Mixed Aviation Corps
    267th Ground Attack Aviation Division
    288th Fighter Aviation Division
282nd Fighter Aviation Division
221st Bomber Aviation Division

208th Ground Attack Aviation Regiment
637th Ground Attack Aviation Regiment
Total operational aircraft: 423, comprising 166 Yak-1 fighters, 118 Pe-2 and Boston bombers, 133 Il-2 Sturmoviks, six reconnaissance aircraft

DON FRONT (GENERAL-POLKOVNIK KONSTANTIN K. ROKOSSOVSKY)

24th Army (General-leytenant Ivan V. Galanin)
49th Rifle Division
84th Rifle Division
120th Rifle Division
173rd Rifle Division
214th Rifle Division
233rd Rifle Division
260th Rifle Division
273rd Rifle Division
298th Rifle Division
10th Tank Brigade
65th Army (General-leytenant Pavel I. Batov)
4th Guards Rifle Division
27th Guards Rifle Division
40th Guards Rifle Division
23rd Rifle Division
24th Rifle Division
252nd Rifle Division
258th Rifle Division
304th Rifle Division
321st Rifle Division
91st Tank Brigade
121st Tank Brigade
66th Army (General-leytenant Aleksei S. Zhadov)
64th Rifle Division
99th Rifle Division
116th Rifle Division
226th Rifle Division
299th Rifle Division
343rd Rifle Division
58th Tank Brigade
Under Front control:
16th Tank Corps (General-major Aleksei G. Maslov)
64th Tank Brigade
148th Tank Brigade
4th Artillery Division
16th Air Army (General-major Sergei I. Rudenko)
220th Fighter Aviation Division
283rd Fighter Aviation Division
228th Ground Attack Aviation Division
291st Ground Attack Aviation Division
271st Night Bomber Aviation Division (83 U-2s)
Total operational aircraft: 203, comprising 56 Yak-1 fighters, 64 Il-2s, 83 U-2s

STALINGRAD FRONT (GENERAL-POLKOVNIK ANDREI I. EREMENKO)

28th Army (General-leytenant Vasily F. Gerasimenko)
34th Guards Rifle Division
248th Rifle Division
52nd Rifle Brigade
152nd Rifle Brigade
159th Rifle Brigade
6th Guards Tank Brigade
51st Army (General-major Nikolai I. Trufanov)
15th Guards Rifle Division
91st Rifle Division
126th Rifle Division
302nd Rifle Division
4th Mechanized Corps (General-major Vasily T. Volskiy)
4th Cavalry Corps (General-leytenant Timofei T. Shapkin)
254th Tank Brigade
38th Separate Motorized Rifle Brigade

57th Army (General-major Fedor I. Tolbukhin)
169th Rifle Division
422nd Rifle Division
143rd Rifle Brigade
13th Tank Corps (General-major Trofim I. Tanaschishin)
90th Tank Brigade
235th Tank Brigade
62nd Army (General-leytenant Vasily I. Chuikov)
13th Guards Rifle Division
37th Guards Rifle Division
39th Guards Rifle Division
45th Rifle Division
95th Rifle Division
112th Rifle Division
138th Rifle Division
193rd Rifle Division
284th Rifle Division
308th Rifle Division
42nd Naval Rifle Brigade
92nd Naval Rifle Brigade
115th Rifle Brigade
124th Rifle Brigade
149th Rifle Brigade
160th Rifle Brigade
84th Tank Brigade
64th Army (General-major Mikhail S. Shumilov)
7th Rifle Corps (General-major Sergei G. Goriachev)
36th Guards Rifle Division
29th Rifle Division
38th Rifle Division
157th Rifle Division
204th Rifle Division
66th Naval Rifle Brigade
154th Naval Rifle Brigade
13th Tank Brigade
56th Tank Brigade
8th Air Army (General-major Timofei T. Khriukhin)
2nd Mixed Aviation Corps
    201st Fighter Aviation Division
    235th Fighter Aviation Division
    214th Ground Attack Aviation Division
268th Fighter Aviation Division
287th Fighter Aviation Division
206th Ground Attack Aviation Division
226th Mixed Aviation Division
289th Mixed Aviation Division
270th Bomber Aviation Division
272nd Night Bomber Aviation Division
Total operational aircraft: 401, comprising 128 fighters (36 La-5s, 68 Yak-1s, 14 Yak-7Bs and 10 LaGG-3s), 171 Il-2s, 22 bombers (SB, Pe-2 and Su-2), 80 U-2 night bombers

AVIATION

102nd Fighter Aviation Division/Stalingrad Protivovozdushnoy Oborony (PVO, Air Defence Command)
Total operational: about 48 fighters, including 15 Hurricanes, 16 Yak-1s and five LaGG-3s.

AXIS

HEERESGRUPPE B (GENERALOBERST MAXIMILIAN VON WEICHS)

6.Armee (General der Panzertruppe Friedrich Paulus)

VIII.Armee-Korps (General der Artillerie Walter Heitz)
76.Infanterie-Division (Generalmajor Carl Rodenburg)
113.Infanterie-Division (Generalleutnant Hans-Heinrich Sixt von Arnim)

XI.Armee-Korps (General der Infanterie Karl Strecker)
44.Infanterie-Division (Generalmajor Heinrich Deboi)
376.Infanterie-Division (Generalmajor Alexander Edler von Daniels)
384.Infanterie-Division (Generalleutnant Eccard Freiherr von Gablenz)
Sturmgeschütz-Abteilung 177 (10 StuG IIIs)
XIV.Panzer-Korps (Generalleutnant Hans Valentin Hube)
3.Infanterie-Division (mot.) (Generalmajor Helmuth Schlömer)
60.Infanterie-Division (mot.) (Generalmajor Otto Kohlermann)
94.Infanterie-Division (Generalleutnant Georg Pfeiffer)
16.Panzer-Division (Generalmajor Günther Angern)
LI.Armee-Korps (General der Artillerie Walter von Seydlitz-Kurzbach)
71.Infanterie-Division (Generalmajor Alexander von Hartmann)
79.Infanterie-Division (Generalmajor Richard Graf von Schwerin)
100.Jäger-Division (Generalleutnant Werner Sanne)
295.Infanterie-Division (Generalmajor Rolf Wuthmann)
305.Infanterie-Division (Oberst Bernhard Steinmetz)
389.Infanterie-Division (Generalleutnant Erwin Jaenecke)
14.Panzer-Division (Generalleutnant Ferdinand Heim)
    Kampfgruppe Seydel
24.Panzer-Division (Generalmajor Arno von Lenski)
Sturmgeschütz-Abteilung 244 (20 StuG IIIs)
Sturmgeschütz-Abteilung 245 (two StuG IIIs)
Under 6.Armee control:
9.Flak-Division (Oberst Wolfgang Pickert)
    Flak-Regiment 37 (four Flak battalions)
    Flak-Regiment 91 (four Flak battalions)
    Flak-Regiment 104 (four Flak battalions)

4.PANZER-ARMEE (GENERALOBERST HERMANN HOTH)

IV.Armee-Korps (General der Pioniere Erwin Jaenecke)
297.Infanterie-Division (Generalleutnant Max Pfeffer)
371.Infanterie-Division (Generalmajor Richard Stempel)
Romanian 20th Infantry Division
Sturmgeschütz-Abteilung 243 (minus 2.Batterie) (seven StuG IIIs)
Romanian VI Army Corps (Lieutenant General Corneliu Dragalina)
Romanian 1st Infantry Division (General de brigadă Ioan D. Mihăescu)
Romanian 2nd Infantry Division (General de brigadă Dumitru I. Tudose)
Romanian 4th Infantry Division (General de brigadă Barbu E. Alinescu)
Romanian 18th Infantry Division
6th Rosiori Regiment (mot.) (5th Cavalry Division)
Romanian VII Army Corps (General Florea Mitranescu)
5th Cavalry Division
8th Cavalry Division
29.Infanterie-Division (mot.) (Generalmajor Hans Leyser)[1]
16.Infanterie-Division (mot.) (Generalmajor Gerhard von Schwerin)[2]

ROMANIAN THIRD ARMY (GENERAL DE ARMATĂ PETRE DUMITRESCU)

I Army Corps (General Teodor Ionescu)
7th Infantry Division
11th Infantry Division
II Army Corps (General Nicolae Dascalescu)
9th Infantry Division
14th Infantry Division

IV Army Corps (General Constantin Sanatescu)
1st Cavalry Division
13th Infantry Division
'Colonel Voicu' detachment[3]
V Army Corps (General Aurelian Son)
5th Infantry Division
6th Infantry Division
15th Infantry Division
XXXXVIII.Panzer-Korps (Generalleutnant Ferdinand Heim)
22.Panzer-Division (Generalmajor Wilhelm von Apell)
Romanian 1st Armoured Division (Major General Radu Gheorghe)
    (131 tanks, comprising 109 R-2s, 11 Panzer III Ausf. N, 11 Panzer IV Ausf. G)
7th Cavalry Division
Kampfgruppe Simon (Oberstleutnant Arnold Simon)[4]
    Panzerjäger-Abteilung 162
Romanian Gruparea Aeriană de Luptă (General Ermil Gheorghiu)
7th Fighter Group (37 Bf 109Es)
8th Fighter Group (36 IAR 80Bs)
6th Fighter-Bomber Group (IAR-81s)
1st Bomber Group (15 Savoia S79s)
3rd Bomber Group (PZL P23Bs, Potez 633s, IAR-37s)
5th Bomber Group (15 He-111s)

LUFTFLOTTE 4 (GENERALOBERST WOLFRAM FREIHERR VON RICHTHOFEN)

VIII.Fliegerkorps (Generalleutnant Martin Fiebig)
Stab., I., III./Jagdgeschwader 3 (40 Bf-109Fs)
I., II./Zerstörergeschwader 1 (33 Bf 110D/E/Fs)
Stab., II., III./Kampfgeschwader 27 (27 He 111s)
Stab., I., II., III./ Schlachtgeschwader 1 (nine Bf 109E-7s, three Hs 123s, eight Hs 129s)
I., II./Sturzkampfgeschwader 2 (42 Ju 87s)
Total: 162–193 operational combat aircraft[5]
Air Transport
KGrzbV. 50 (13x Ju-52)
KGrzbV. 900 (12x Ju-52)

REINFORCEMENTS

26 November 1942
1./Pz. Abt. 301 (FKL) or Kompanie Abendroth (11 Panzer III Ausf. J)
28 November 1942
336.Infanterie-Division
6.Panzer-Division
7 December 1942
11.Panzer-Division
9 December 1942
7.Luftwaffen-Feld-Division
10 December 1942
23.Panzer-Division
15 December 1942
304.Infanterie-Division
306.Infanterie-Division
8.Luftwaffen-Feld-Division
17 December 1942
17.Panzer-Division

---

1   Although assigned to XXXXVIII.Panzer-Korps on 10 November, the division remained in the 4.Panzer-Armee sector as an operational-level reserve.
2   The division was assigned to screen the Kalmyk steppe near Elista.
3   This detachment consisted of three Romanian infantry battalions, one Romanian artillery battalion and the German Panzerjäger-Abteilung (Sfl) 611 (14 Marder IIs).
4   The Kampfgruppe had about 950 soldiers and also included a bicycle-mounted reconnaissance battalion and a mixed artillery battalion equipped with 10cm guns and 15cm howitzers.
5   Some sources claim that VIII.Fliegerkorps may have had up to 193 operational combat aircraft.

OPPOSING PLANS

SOVIET

The genesis of the eventual Soviet victory at Stalingrad lay in the gradual recognition that previous counter-offensives by the Red Army in southern Russia in 1942 had failed to achieve surprise or mass sufficient combat power to break the enemy's front. Although General Georgy Zhukov later claimed in his memoirs that he was the first to suggest a broad envelopment of 6.Armee at Stalingrad, it was actually General-polkovnik Andrei I. Eremenko, commander of the Stalingrad Front, who raised the idea with Stavka in early October 1942. It was Eremenko, the man on the spot, who had been forced to conduct three unsuccessful Soviet counter-offensives in the Kotluban sector in August and September 1942. However, Paulus' 6.Armee had created an efficient kill zone around Kotluban, which shredded one Soviet attack after another. Eremenko recognized that the predictability of these attacks and the ability of the Luftwaffe to intervene over the battlefield deprived the Red Army of any real chance of success under these conditions. Something different was needed.

By late September 1942, the GKO and Stavka in Moscow were already developing plans for several possible winter counter-offensives, although only in broad-brush fashion. Zhukov, whom Stalin had recently made deputy-commander-in-chief of the Red Army, favoured a pincer offensive by the Kalinin and Western fronts against the German-held Rzhev salient. He argued that a pincer attack by the two fronts could cut off and destroy the German 9.Armee in the salient, thereby achieving a decisive operational-level victory. As for Stalingrad, Zhukov recommended more offensives to batter away at 6.Armee's flanks, but not radically different from previous operations. However, Eremenko arrived in Moscow for planning meetings on 6 October and suggested a new approach: instead of repeating the same methods as used in previous unsuccessful attacks against 6.Armee's left flank, Eremenko recommended a broad envelopment of 6.Armee, with powerful strike groups attacking from both the north and south, converging upon Kalach. Eremenko argued that Rokossovsky's Don Front could use its bridgehead over the Don in the Kremenskaya sector to attack the Romanian Third Army, while the 51st and 57th armies could attack the mixed German–Romanian force in the Lake Sarpa sector. He pointed out that the enemy was less likely to expect a major attack in these relatively quiet sectors, and that consequently fewer mobile reserves could be expected to be on hand.

It was Eremenko (seated), not Zhukov or the General Staff in Moscow, who initially developed the concept for a broad envelopment of 6.Armee at Stalingrad, rather than just continuing to pound on the enemy's well-defended northern flank. Nikita S. Khrushchev, a member of the Stalingrad Military Council, also helped ensure that Stalin learned about Eremenko's concept for a 'new approach' at Stalingrad. (Author's collection)

The idea of attacking less-capable Romanian units was also appealing, since Axis satellite troops were assessed to be poorly equipped and less motivated. Stalin took an interest in Eremenko's concept, so Stavka began refining the concept into an operational plan. Zhukov was less impressed by the concept, and simply ordered Eremenko to keep pounding 6.Armee in the Kotluban sector; on 15–16 October, he issued directives for another attack in the same area as before. Rokossovsky's Don Front was provided with several fresh rifle divisions and was ordered to attack again in the Kotluban sector. Unsurprisingly, Hube's alert XIV.Panzer-Korps held firm and knocked out 86 Soviet tanks in two days of heavy fighting on 20 and 21 October. The Fourth Kotluban Offensive was another failure that squandered Soviet lives and equipment for negligible gain. Furthermore, heavy losses forced Rokossovsky to disband no fewer than seven of his shattered rifle divisions.

As Stavka transformed Operation *Uranus* from a concept into a plan, measures were taken to prepare for the offensive. In late October, a new South-Western Front was created in order to spearhead the offensive, and General-leytenant Nikolai F. Vatutin was brought in to lead this formation. Vatutin was provided with the 1st Guards Army and the rebuilt 5th Tank Army, both led by veteran commanders. Sensing that Stalin favoured *Uranus*, Zhukov and the rest of Stavka decided to endorse the idea that the Red Army was now powerful enough to launch two near-simultaneous major winter counter-offensives, one at Rzhev and one at Stalingrad. The Rzhev offensive was designated as Operation *Mars* and would start about one week after Operation *Uranus*, in the hope that German reserves would be withdrawn from Heeresgruppe Mitte to reinforce Heeresgruppe B. Zhukov and General-polkovnik Aleksandr M. Vasilevskiy, chief of the Soviet General Staff, personally oversaw the planning for both *Mars* and *Uranus*. Furthermore, Stavka began planning two follow-on operations, named *Jupiter* and *Saturn*, which would exploit any success achieved by *Mars* and *Uranus*. Initially, *Mars* and *Uranus* were expected to begin by late October, but were delayed twice and slipped to late November.

experience from the previous winter, the Germans knew that the Red Army was likely to launch one or more winter counter-offensives to try to retake ground lost during the summer months, but they misjudged where this might occur. Oberst Reinhard Gehlen's Fremde Heere Ost (FHO, Foreign Armies East), the intelligence department within the OKH, was responsible for assessing likely enemy courses of action. Gehlen concluded that the Soviets were most likely to launch their main winter counter-offensive against Heeresgruppe Mitte (Centre), either against 9.Armee in the Rzhev salient or 2.Panzer-Armee in the Orel sector. While Gehlen's intelligence estimate of 18 November noted that aerial reconnaissance and signals intercepts had detected Soviet reinforcements moving more forces into the bridgeheads opposite the Romanian Third Army, he did not see this as a major threat. Instead, German reconnaissance completely failed to detect the presence of the 5th Tank Army near the Don bridgeheads. Consequently, Gehlen's anodyne assessment issued only a vague warning that the Soviets might make a limited-scale offensive either west or south of Stalingrad, but not in both places. Gehlen arrogantly assumed that since earlier Soviet counter-offensives against 6.Armee had been contained, any future enemy offensive could also be repulsed. As a result of Gehlen's erroneous intelligence estimate, the OKH positioned nine of its 19 *Panzer-Divisionen* with over half the operational armour in the Heeresgruppe Mitte sector. Heeresgruppe B was left with only one-quarter of available German armour, virtually all of it in close proximity to Stalingrad.

Despite Gehlen's confident intelligence assessment, Hitler was not blind to the possibility that the Soviets might attempt to attack the Romanian-held sectors. At one of his daily conferences at Werwolf in Vinnitsa on 26 October, Hitler directed that three divisions in France, including the rebuilt 6.Panzer-Division, should be sent to reinforce the Romanian sector. However, the OKH staff did not make this a priority and the divisions did not arrive until after Operation *Uranus* had begun. Although Hitler was often guilty of micro-management, on this occasion it would have been justified. In addition, Hitler wanted some of the new *Luftwaffen-Feld-Divisionen*, authorized in late September, to be assigned to the Romanian and Italian armies to stiffen them. One week before Operation *Uranus* began, Hitler decided to return to Berchtesgaden for a brief holiday, which reduced his situational awareness at a key moment.

At von Weichs' Heeresgruppe B headquarters near Starobelsk, there was growing apprehension about the Don Front, but little that could be done. General Petre Dumitrescu, commander of the Romanian Third Army, was particularly nervous about the ability of his command to withstand a major Soviet attack. He requested additional anti-tank guns and anti-tank mines, so Heeresgruppe B provided 60 7.5cm Pak 97/38 anti-tank guns. Dumitrescu complained that this was not enough. On 10 November, Heeresgruppe B reassigned Generalleutnant Ferdinand Heim's XXXXVIII. Panzer-Korps from 4.Panzer-Armee to serve as a mobile reserve behind the Romanian Third Army. In the event of an enemy breakthrough in the Romanian sector, Heim was expected to counter-attack with 22.Panzer-Division, the Romanian 1st Armoured Division and the Romanian 7th Cavalry Division. Von Weichs knew that Heim's mobile reserve, based upon an incomplete *Panzer-Division* and obsolete Romanian tanks, had very limited combat value, but sought to calm Dumitrescu's concerns.

THE CAMPAIGN

OPERATION *URANUS*, 19–23 NOVEMBER 1942

The men in the forward positions of the Romanian Third Army knew that a Soviet offensive was imminent, since the South-Western Front had ordered aggressive night reconnaissance patrols a week prior to *Uranus*. By the night of 17/18 November, the Soviet patrols had escalated to battalion-size probes, which identified Romanian combat outposts and began removing mines and other obstacles in the primary attack sectors. While these preliminary Soviet actions alerted the Romanians – who notified Heeresgruppe B – they did serve to compromise the enemy's forward outpost line prior to the start of the offensive. Nevertheless, weather conditions were so miserable – with visibility limited to 200m or less – that Soviet commanders briefly considered postponing the offensive for another day, before opting to continue.

At 0730hrs on 19 November, the South-Western and Don fronts began an 80-minute artillery preparation against the enemy positions. Although the Soviet artillery and rocket barrages were impressive, the heavy ground fog and falling snow made it impossible for forward observers to adjust fires, so the artillerymen simply fired against known or suspected positions. Nor was the VVS able to fly its strike sorties until later in the day, due to poor flying weather. In fact, the Soviet artillery preparation inflicted only modest damage on the Romanian Third Army. At 0840hrs, Soviet shock groups began moving forward even before the artillery preparation had lifted, with infantrymen clad in white snowsuits in the lead. In the west, Romanenko's 5th Tank Army began its assault, with four tank–infantry shock groups from four rifle divisions (14th Guards Rifle Division, 47th Guards Rifle Division, 50th Guards Rifle Division and 119th Rifle Division). The 47th Guards Rifle Division, supported by 64 tanks, tore into the Romanian 14th Infantry Division. Likewise, the 50th Guards Rifle Division, supported by 74 tanks, caused the Romanian 5th Infantry Division to buckle. However, the 14th Guards Rifle Division attacked without tank support and was repulsed by heavy defensive fire from the Romanian 9th Infantry Division. The centre of the Romanian Third Army, anchored on the town of Blinov, held for the moment. Despite denting the Romanian defences, the initial attacks of the 5th Tank Army did not achieve an immediate breakthrough, and by 1100hrs the shock groups had advanced no more than 2–3km. The situation was much the same with General-major Ivan M. Chistiakov's 21st Army, which attacked the right wing of the Romanian Third Army with three rifle divisions

(63rd, 76th and 293rd), each supported by a regiment of KV-1 heavy tanks. Although the Soviet shock groups were able to overrun part of the Romanian 13th Infantry Division, they did not achieve an immediate breakthrough either. Finally, General-leytenant Pavel I. Batov's 65th Army from the Don Front launched a supporting attack with two rifle divisions (27th Guards Rifle Division, 304th Rifle Division) against the boundary between the Romanian Third Army and Strecker's XI.Armee-Korps, but failed to achieve any real progress. Resistance from the German 376.Infanterie-Division was particularly tough and blocked any Soviet advance against the left flank of 6.Armee.

Dumitrescu's Third Army immediately called for help to prevent a Soviet breakthrough, but the Germans proved unusually slow to react. It was not until 1030hrs – three hours after the beginning of the Soviet artillery preparation – that Heim's XXXXVIII.Panzer-Korps began to move northwards. The plan was that 22.Panzer-Division would link up with the Romanian 1st Armoured Division, and together they would move against the 21st Army's shock groups attacking the Romanian right wing. However, Hitler intervened at 1150hrs and ordered Heim to instead counter-attack the Soviet shock groups near Blinov, threatening to break the Romanian centre. Hitler's decision was essentially correct, in that 5th Guards Tank Army was a greater threat than the 21st Army, but this last-minute intervention only added further friction and delay to the German response. Fuel shortages and icy roads further delayed Heim's XXXXVIII.Panzer-Korps.

Annoyed by the failure of their shock groups to achieve a rapid breakthrough, both Romanenko and Chistiakov decided around 1200hrs to commit their armour–cavalry mobile groups to overwhelm the Romanian defences before German assistance could arrive. In Romanenko's sector, the 1st and 26th Tank corps moved forward and smashed into the centre of the Romanian line just east of Blinov. The sudden appearance of nearly 200 tanks led to the complete collapse of the Romanian 14th Infantry Division. General-major Vasily V. Butkov's 1st Tank Corps surged southwards, ploughing through the wreckage of the Romanian centre. General-major Mikhail D. Borisov's 8th Cavalry Corps soon joined the advance and assisted in overrunning several enemy-occupied villages. By late afternoon, the Romanian centre was shattered and Romanenko's spearheads had advanced about 10km from the start line – which was well short of the expected progress. Chistiakov enjoyed more success in his sector, where General-major Andrei G. Kravchenko's 4th Tank Corps achieved a significant breakthrough, and two of its brigades managed to advance nearly 20km in three hours. General-major Issa A. Pliev's 3rd Guards Cavalry Corps followed, further widening the breach. The Romanian 15th Infantry Division, which had been held in tactical reserve, moved forward to prop up the crumbling 13th Infantry Division, thereby preventing a complete collapse. Kampfgruppe Simon also moved to support the Romanians, and its Panzerjägers destroyed 11 Soviet tanks. However, the 21st Army was now in a good position to exploit southwards, and by nightfall its advance units were across the Kurtlak River and approaching Manoylin, 35km south of Kletskaya.

The Romanian V Army Corps was still solid in the centre with its three infantry divisions, but both its flanks were bent back by the advance of the Soviet 5th Guards Tank Army and 21st Army. Late in the day, the weather improved slightly and VIII.Fliegerkorps managed to generate some strike sorties, which destroyed 11 pontoon bridges over the Don. However, the Luftwaffe could not intervene effectively over the battlefield and the only hope remaining for the Axis was Heim's XXXXVIII.Panzer-Korps. Instead of striking the Soviet armoured spearheads with a concentrated force, Heim's Panzer-Korps stumbled into action, with vehicles short of fuel and the Romanians and Germans unable to coordinate with each other. Kampfgruppe Oppeln (under Oberst Hermann von Oppeln-Bronikowski) from 22.Panzer-Division conducted a meeting engagement against Butkov's 1st Tank Corps, leading to a wild, night tank action near Peschanyi around 1700hrs. Oppeln-Bronikowski only had about 30 operational tanks, one battalion of motorized infantry and a few small support units, but he did succeed in halting the enemy advance. Further eastwards, the Romanian 1st Armoured Division bumped into Soviet infantry and tanks near Zhirkovskiy, leading to another swirling fight. Given that much of the Soviet infantry

Soviet infantry attack, while over-watched by a DPM light machine gunner. Note one soldier falling just after leaving the trench. Typical Soviet rifle units in late 1942 did not possess a great deal of firepower and mobility, which limited their ability to keep up with mechanized units. (Author's collection)

The 5th Tank Army broke through the Romanian Third Army by committing its armour en masse, which overwhelmed the anaemic enemy anti-tank defences. However, contrary to Soviet claims, the Romanians did not rout, and thus the 5th Tank Army was unable to achieve its operational objectives on the first two days of the offensive. (Nik Cornish at www.Stavka.org.uk)

in the 5th Guards Tank Army was still engaged in mopping up Romanian infantry positions, the Soviet tank–cavalry exploitation force initially lacked the combat power to overwhelm the XXXXVIII.Panzer-Korps elements. Nevertheless, by the end of the day, Dumitrescu's Third Army was pierced in two places and the Axis tactical reserves were unable to reverse the situation.

At 6.Armee headquarters, Paulus was not unduly alarmed by initial reports of the Soviet offensive and expected Heim's XXXXVIII.Panzer-Korps to be able to contain any breakthrough. In addition, the *Kampfgruppe* from 14.Panzer-Division seemed adequate to assist General der Infanterie Karl Strecker's XI.Armee-Korps in maintaining a solid left flank. Yet as the day progressed and reports of Soviet tanks punching holes through the Romanian front reached Paulus, he became alarmed and began issuing orders to transfer elements of Hube's XIV.Panzer-Korps to his left flank. Both 16.Panzer-Division and 24.Panzer-Division were ordered to send *Kampfgruppen* across the Don bridges to prevent Soviet tanks from reaching 6.Armee's lines of communication. Once his panzers were assembled west of the Don, Hube was expected to launch a coordinated counter-attack to eliminate the Soviet spearheads. In order to move Hube's corps, the 6.Armee quartermasters were obliged to expend their small fuel reserves. Extracting units from fighting around Stalingrad also proved more time-consuming than expected, which meant that Hube required nearly two days to assemble his forces for a counter-stroke. However, these last-minute gestures proved futile, since Eremenko's Stalingrad Front was just about to launch its own offensive in a few hours, which would push the situation past retrieval for 6.Armee.

On the morning of 20 November, both the South-Western and Don fronts continued their offensives, seeking to widen the breaches in the Romanian front. In the centre, Butkov's 1st Tank Corps wasted much of the day sparring with Kampfgruppe Oppeln. Romanenko ordered Butkov to bypass this resistance and continue south, but this did not occur. Instead, both forces continued to pound away at each other; Butkov lost about 50 of his 136 tanks in the first two days of *Uranus*, while Oppeln-Bronikowski was down to about 20 tanks. Meanwhile, Borisov's 8th Cavalry Corps succeeded in slipping around Kampfgruppe Oppeln and moved off to the south-west. In the process, Borisov bumped into the Romanian 7th Cavalry Division and routed it – further widening the hole in the Romanian centre. Rodin's 26th Tank Corps fought the Romanian 1st Armoured Division along the Tsaritsa River. The Romanians tried to break through to link up with 22.Panzer-Division but lost 25 tanks in the attempt. Rodin eventually managed to detach two brigades from the fighting by late morning and they drove southwards, capturing Perelazovskiy by noon. The loss of this town left the Romanian 1st Armoured Division nearly isolated and they began withdrawing to the east. Even more serious, the three infantry divisions (5th, 6th and 15th) of the Romanian V Corps were now being enveloped on both flanks and threatened with encirclement. General Mihail Lascar, commander of the 6th Infantry Division, took charge of this force, which was now dubbed 'Group Lascar'. Lascar's position was dangerous, but his troops were still solid and they maintained their positions. Indeed, Group Lascar could have attempted to escape to the south, but von Weichs ordered it to remain in place and await relief from Heim's XXXXVIII.Panzer-Korps. Chistiakov's 21st Army enveloped Lascar's right flank with part of his forces while sending Kravchenko's 4th Tank Corps to advance to the south-east, albeit with just two brigades. Pliev's 3rd Guards Cavalry Corps also joined the push south. Surprisingly, remnants of the Romanian IV Corps continued to fight and delay the bulk of Chistiakov's army along the Kurtlak River, which prevented a rapid exploitation of the situation. Indeed, Chistiakov was concerned that Panzers from 6.Armee might arrive at any moment and demolish his mobile group while it was spread out. Although the Romanian Third Army had taken significant damage, most units were still fighting and the Soviets had not taken any large hauls of Axis prisoners.

Batov's 65th Army continued its supporting attacks against the left flank of the German XI.Armee-Korps. Although a *Kampfgruppe* from 14.Panzer-Division was guarding the open flank, one of Batov's rifle divisions achieved a small penetration in the sector held by the Romanian 1st Cavalry Division. Displaying admirable flexibility, Batov formed a mobile group with 40 tanks and four battalions of motorized rifle troops under Polkovnik Georgy I. Anisimov, then sent it to exploit the penetration. Amazingly, Anisimov's ad hoc mobile group advanced 23km into the rear of XI.Armee-Korps, sparking a panic among the support troops. The Germans were now getting a taste of the 'tank panic' their own rapid panzer advances had caused in 1939–41 and the effect was similar.

While the Axis struggled to contain the attacks of the South-Western and Don fronts, the Stalingrad Front began its own offensive against Hoth's forces south of the city on the morning of 20 November. Once again, the mix of snow and fog severely limited visibility, and Eremenko decided to allow his three army commanders to commence their own operations when weather conditions in their sectors improved. Trufanov's 51st Army attacked first, with a 60-minute artillery preparation followed by a ground assault with three rifle divisions (126th and 302nd Rifle divisions, and 15th Guards Rifle Division) and 80 tanks. The Romanian VI Corps was extremely thin in the sector south of Lake Sarpa with just five infantry battalions facing Trufanov's three shock groups. Inevitably, the weak Romanian defence crumbled quickly and Trufanov's troops took 2,500 prisoners. However, for a variety of reasons, Trufanov was slow to get Volskiy's 4th Mechanized Corps into action. It was not until 1300hrs that the mechanized group began

AXIS

1. 371.Infanterie-Division
2. 297.Infanterie-Division
3. 20th Infantry Division (Romanian)
4. 2nd Infantry Division (Romanian)
5. 18th Infantry Division (Romanian)
6. 1st Infantry Division (Romanian)
7. 4th Infantry Division (Romanian)
8. 29.Infanterie-Division (mot.)
9. 4.Panzer-Armee headquarters
10. Engineer Battalion, 18th Infantry Division (Romanian)
11. 6th Rosiori Regiment/5th Cavalry Division (Romanian)
12. Kampfgruppe von Hanstein

XXX
VI

DRAGALINA

N

KALACH

KARPOVKA RIVER

DON RIVER

M

BRIDGE OUT

16

BUZINOVK

XXX
IV

JAENECKE

MYSHKOVA RIVER

VERKHNE TSARITSYNSKY

14 9

ABGANERO

AKSAI RIVER

11   7

AKSAI

EVENTS

20 November 1942

1. 0830hrs: After a heavy artillery bombardment, the 51st Army attacks with the 15th Guards Rifle Division north of Lake Tsatsa and the 126th Rifle Division and 302nd Rifle Division between Lake Tsatsa and Lake Barmantsak. The right flank of the Romanian 18th Infantry Division and the left flank of the Romanian 1st Infantry Division are routed after less than three hours of fighting.

2. 1115hrs: The 57th Army attacks with two rifle divisions, one rifle brigade and 40 tanks, rupturing the Romanian lines in this sector in less than one hour.

3. 1300hrs: The 51st Army commits the 4th Mechanized Corps, which advances west. While part of the corps reduces Romanian resistance in Plodovitoye, two other mobile groups continue west towards the main rail line.

4. 1420hrs: The 64th Army attacks with three rifle divisions and 40 tanks. The left flank penetrates the Romanian 20th Infantry Division, but the left flank attack is repulsed by the German 297.Infanterie-Division.

5. 1500hrs: The German 29.Infanterie-Division (mot.) conducts a limited counter-attack against the 422nd Rifle Division, which has little effect.

6. 1620hrs: The 13th Tank Corps is committed and it advances towards Koshary.

7. An attempted counter-attack by the Romanian Rosiori Regiment fails.

8. 2200hrs: The 4th Cavalry Corps follows the 4th Mechanized Corps and pushes towards Abganerovo.

9. Night: Most of the troops of the isolated Romanian 2nd Infantry Division surrender.

21 November 1942

10. 0430hrs: The German 29.Infanterie-Division (mot.) engages the 13th Tank Corps in a protracted meeting engagement near Koshary.

11. The 64th Army attempts to finish off the Romanian 20th Infantry Division and advance to Nariman, but is halted by fierce resistance from the German 29.Infanterie-Division (mot.).

12. 1600–1700hrs: The 4th Mechanized Corps captures Tinguta station, then Zety.

13. 1600hrs: One brigade from the 4th Mechanized Corps and the 4th Cavalry Corps captures Abganerovo station. The 126th and 302nd Rifle divisions follow, pushing south.

14. Evening: Hoth moves his headquarters back to Buzinovka, then west of the Don.

22 November 1942

15. Due to the envelopment by 4th Mechanized Corps, the Germans are forced to create a new line anchored on Tsybenko, Karpovka and Marinovka.

16. 0600hrs: The 4th Mechanized Corps advances north-west and reaches Sovetskiy farm by 1220hrs. The link-up with the South-Western Front will occur here at 1600hrs the next day.

17. The 57th Army captures Nariman and advances towards Tsybenko.

18. 1300hrs: Reinforced by the 36th Guards Rifle Division, the 64th Army attacks and pushes back the right flank of the IV.Armee-Korps.

19. Evening: The 4th Mechanized Corps attempts to take Karpovka, but is repulsed by Kampfgruppe von Hanstein, which arrives just in time.

OPERATION *URANUS*, STALINGRAD FRONT, 20–22 NOVEMBER 1942

The Stalingrad Front launched its offensive one day after the South-Western and Don fronts began their attacks in Operation *Uranus*. Eremenko attacked with three armies against Hoth's right flank, which was held primarily by the German IV.Armee-Korps and the Romanian VI Corps.

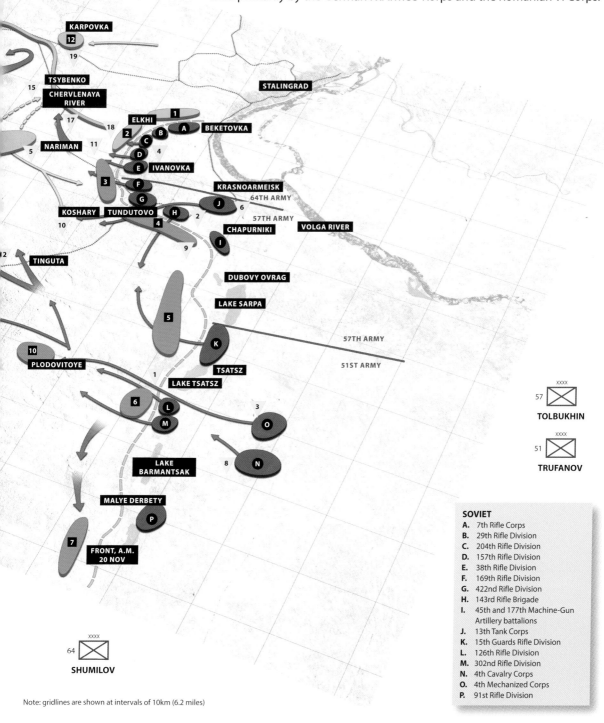

KARPOVKA
12
19
TSYBENKO
15
CHERVLENAYA RIVER
STALINGRAD
17
18
ELKHI
1
2
B
A
BEKETOVKA
C
NARIMAN
11
D
4
E
IVANOVKA
3
F
KRASNOARMEISK
64TH ARMY
G
J
KOSHARY
TUNDUTOVO
H
6
10
4
2
57TH ARMY
CHAPURNIKI
VOLGA RIVER
9
I
TINGUTA
DUBOVY OVRAG
LAKE SARPA
5
57TH ARMY
K
51ST ARMY
10
PLODOVITOYE
TSATSZ
1
LAKE TSATSZ
6
L
3
M
O
LAKE BARMANTSAK
8
N
MALYE DERBETY
P
7
FRONT, A.M. 20 NOV

57
XXXX
TOLBUKHIN

51
XXXX
TRUFANOV

64
XXXX
SHUMILOV

SOVIET
A. 7th Rifle Corps
B. 29th Rifle Division
C. 204th Rifle Division
D. 157th Rifle Division
E. 38th Rifle Division
F. 169th Rifle Division
G. 422nd Rifle Division
H. 143rd Rifle Brigade
I. 45th and 177th Machine-Gun Artillery battalions
J. 13th Tank Corps
K. 15th Guards Rifle Division
L. 126th Rifle Division
M. 302nd Rifle Division
N. 4th Cavalry Corps
O. 4th Mechanized Corps
P. 91st Rifle Division

Note: gridlines are shown at intervals of 10km (6.2 miles)

moving forward, and then its progress was ponderous, manoeuvring around uncleared minefields and dealing with a Romanian–German reserve position in the village of Plodovitoye. Trufanov would not let Volskiy get bogged down in reducing an isolated position and ordered him to dispatch two brigade-size mobile groups to capture Abganerovo and Tinguta stations. Tolbukhin's 57th Army launched its ground attack with two rifle divisions, a rifle brigade and 54 tanks at 1115hrs, which achieved a clean breakthrough. The Romanian 2nd Infantry Division was quickly isolated and forced to surrender, leaving nothing left to plug the large hole in the front. Shumilov's 64th Army, in the Beketovka salient, attacked last at 1420hrs. Shumilov concentrated two rifle divisions and 20 tanks to overwhelm the right regiment of the Romanian 20th Infantry Division. However Shumilov's attack against the German 297.Infanterie-Division failed to gain any ground. Nevertheless, the rapid Romanian collapse allowed Shumilov to commit his own exploitation group, General-major Trofim I. Tanaschishin's 13th Tank Corps, by 1620hrs. Tanaschishin's corps pushed forward towards Koshary, which threatened to turn IV.Armee-Korps' right flank.

Once Hoth learned that Eremenko's forces were attacking the Romanian VI Corps, he ordered Generalmajor Hans Leyser's 29.Infanterie-Division (mot.) to prepare a counter-attack. Leyser dispatched a *Kampfgruppe* built on his *Panzer-Abteilung* and two Panzergrenadier battalions and sent them eastwards, seeking the enemy. Around 1500hrs, the German *Kampfgruppe* encountered some enemy infantry from the 169th Rifle Division south-west of Ivanovka and forced them back. The German panzers also relieved one isolated Romanian position and destroyed eight Soviet tanks in a skirmish, but the commitment of the only full-strength German mobile division in the 6.Armee sector proved remarkably ineffective. Tanaschishin's 13th Tank Corps bypassed Leyser's division and advanced 15km to the south-west. Even worse, Volskiy's 4th Mechanized Corps was gathering momentum and pushing westwards against minimal resistance. Here and there, mines and occasional batteries of German 8.8cm Flak guns inflicted some delay and some casualties, but the Soviet exploitation could not be stopped. Three Romanian divisions had been smashed and Hoth's right flank was crumbling, which Leyser's sole division could not correct on its own. Nevertheless, Leyser's division advanced towards Koshary, and before dawn on 21 November they unexpectedly ran into a tank regiment from Volskiy's 4th Mechanized Corps. In a protracted tank battle, the Germans knocked out 18 Soviet tanks but lost five of their own.

Meanwhile, Hitler, who had just transferred his headquarters from the Wolfsschanze in East Prussia to Berchtesgaden, was belatedly informed by Gehlen's FHO that the previously undetected 5th Tank Army was leading the Soviet offensive out of the Don River bridgeheads. Hitler recognized the threat to Heeresgruppe B, but doubted that von Weichs could handle a real crisis. Consequently, on the evening of 20 November he ordered Generalfeldmarschall Erich von Manstein (who was currently in Vitebsk with his 11.Armee staff) to proceed south to Rostov and, once there, to form Heeresgruppe Don. Hitler directed that 6.Armee, Hoth's forces and the remaining Romanian units would all fall under von Manstein's command. Other divisions, en route from Western Europe, would be provided to von Manstein as they arrived. Hitler had great faith in von Manstein's ability to complete difficult tasks, although the scale of the task was not yet apparent.

While von Manstein and his staff proceeded south, Paulus struggled to shift Hube's XIV.Panzer-Korps west of the Don, but suddenly 6.Armee found itself with insufficient fuel reserves. One *Kampfgruppe* from 24.Panzer-Division crossed the Don to support Strecker's XI.Armee-Korps, but the rest of Hube's forces were still east of the river. While Paulus worried about the threat to his left flank, von Weichs worried about the Soviet breakthrough in Hoth's sector. Once it was clear that the Stalingrad Front had broken through the Romanian VI Corps, von Weichs ordered Hoth to cancel any further counter-attacks by Leyser's 29.Infanterie-Division (mot.)

A platoon of 47mm Bohler anti-tank guns lie silent in the snow, along with their dead crews. Each Romanian infantry regiment had an anti-tank company equipped with 47mm guns, which could not penetrate the frontal armour on Soviet T-34s. Note that the guns are deployed in the open on the steppe, devoid of any kind of cover or concealment. (Süddeutsche Zeitung, Bild 02891402)

and to use it to anchor the right flank of IV.Armee-Korps. Aside from the isolated Group Lascar, the other remnants of the Romanian Third Army and XXXXVIII.Panzer-Korps began falling back toward the Chir River. Although intended to preserve units from encirclement, the Axis movements to protect their flanks tended to make it easier for the Soviet mobile groups to advance into vacated terrain.

By the morning of 21 November, the outcome of Operation *Uranus* was moving inexorably against the Axis. Romanenko's 5th Tank Army had advanced less than half the distance expected, mainly due to the unanticipated resistance of 22.Panzer-Division and Group Lascar, but this could not continue. Borisov's 8th Cavalry Corps gradually enveloped the diminutive 22.Panzer-Division – now down to just a dozen tanks – and finally forced it to retreat towards the Chir River. With this obstacle removed, Butkov's 1st Tank Corps managed to advance about 10km, but the Luftwaffe suddenly appeared over the battlefield when the weather briefly cleared. The VIII. Fliegerkorps managed to fly about 200 strike sorties in support of XXXXVIII. Panzer-Korps, which inflicted significant losses on Butkov's stalled 1st Tank Corps. Rodin's 26th Tank Corps had a better day; after refueling, it moved 65km to the south-west under cover of a snowstorm, encountering only feeble resistance from small Romanian detachments. Incredibly, Rodin's advance guard reached Skvorin, only 20km from Kalach, by evening. Chistiakov's 21st Army also pushed west from the Kletskaya bridgehead to meet rifle units from the 5th Tank Army. By 2000hrs, Group Lascar, including the Romanian 1st Armoured Division, was surrounded by six Soviet rifle divisions from 5th Tank Army and the 21st Army. Chistiakov's 21st Army continued to pound on Strecker's XI.Armee-Korps, with infantry and Pliev's 3rd Guards Cavalry Corps, while Kravchenko's 4th Tank Corps skirted around the open enemy flank and reached the Liska River. Kampfgruppe Dörnemann, consisting of two battalions from 16.Panzer-Division, unsuccessfully tried to stop Kravchenko's tanks from reaching the Don. In a brisk tank action west of the Don, the 4th Tank Corps lost 16 tanks but ten German tanks were knocked out. A larger *Kampfgruppe* from 24.Panzer-Division managed to briefly hold up Pliev's cavalrymen at Sukhanov before falling back. The fog of war also

CAPTURE OF THE BRIDGE AT KALACH, 0830HRS, 22 NOVEMBER 1942 (PP. 36–37)

The primary objective of Operation *Uranus* was to capture a bridge over the Don in order to enable a link up between the armoured spearheads of the South-Western and Stalingrad fronts. By the evening of 21/22 November, the third day of the Soviet offensive, Rodin's 26th Tank Corps was within striking distance of Kalach. The situation around Kalach was highly fluid, with Soviet armoured units probing towards the Don bridges, but uncertain about German forces in the area. Rodin decided to form an advance detachment under Podpolkovnik Georgy N. Filippov, commander of the 14th Motorized Rifle Brigade, to move forward and try to capture an intact bridge over the Don. Filippov's detachment consisted of five T-34 tanks, two motorized rifle companies in trucks, five armoured cars and three captured German armoured vehicles. Filippov set off at 0300hrs and travelled 23km before dawn. Unknown to Filippov, the pontoon bridge was located 4km north-west of Kalach, near the village of Berezovskii. After discovering that the original bridge at Kalach was down, Filippov was tipped off by a local peasant about the intact pontoon bridge. Filippov redirected his column, with the German vehicles at the front, and headed towards Berezovskii.

Although the German commander in the area, Oberst Hans Mikosch, had ordered the pontoon bridge rigged for demolition, he had no real combat units to defend the crossing site. Instead, the bridge was guarded by a Feldgendarmerie (military police) detachment, a single 8.8cm Flak gun and an armed Organization Todt (O.T) construction unit. A Pionier school and numerous rear-echelon support troops were nearby, but not deployed

for defence or even aware that Soviet armoured units were in the vicinity.

Around 0830hrs, Filippov's detachment reached the approaches to the bridge, trying to pass themselves off as a German column. Visibility was poor and the German personnel near the bridge were not particularly alert. Even when a T-34 tank was spotted, the Feldgendarmerie thought it was a captured vehicle, for use in training at the Pionier school. By the time that the Germans finally realized their error, Filippov's men were already on the bridge.

This scene shows the moment when Soviet infantrymen leapt from the captured Panzer III tank in the lead (**1**) and following vehicles to engage the handful of guards. The Germans were caught completely by surprise. The 8.8cm Flak gun (**2**) belatedly got into action and destroyed two T-34s, but the bridge was captured intact and Filippov's men quickly removed the demolition charges. Filippov then formed a defensive perimeter around the pontoon bridge and informed Rodin via radio that he had accomplished his mission. Oberst Mikosch tried to organize a counter-attack to recapture the bridge, but his improvised and poorly armed combat teams were repulsed three times. Filippov was awarded the Hero of the Soviet Union for this coup, and the loss of the bridge at Kalach severed 6.Armee's lines of communication. Reinforcements soon arrived, which used the bridgehead to clear the enemy out of Kalach and then pushed east to link up with the 4th Mechanized Corps approaching from the east.

hindered Hube's ability to identify the enemy spearheads and coordinate his scattered *Kampfgruppen* at the optimum time and place. Consequently, the piecemeal commitment of Hube's small battlegroups proved little more than a hindrance to the Soviet advance, which was now within 20km of Paulus' 6.Armee headquarters at Golubinskaya. As a result, Paulus decided to evacuate this position and move his headquarters to Nizhne-Chirskaya, on the west bank of the Don.

In the south, Leyser's 29.Infanterie-Division (mot.) mounted fierce resistance, which halted Shumilov's 64th Army, but Tolbukhin's 57th Army was gradually slipping around the open flank with Tanaschishin's 13th Tank Corps. Hoth was forced to relocate his headquarters first to Buzinovka, then back to join Paulus at Nizhne-Chirskaya. Trufanov's 51st Army made excellent progress, with Volskiy's 4th Mechanized Corps advancing over 35km to the west, while the two divisions of General-leytenant Timofei T. Shapkin's 4th Cavalry Corps moved south-west to seize Abganerovo station. In addition to capturing stockpiles of supplies, Trufanov's mobile groups took 600 Romanian prisoners. By this point, the Romanian 6th Corps only had elements of two cavalry divisions still in the fight. Kampfgruppe Sauvant (Major Bernhard Sauvant) from 14.Panzer-Division was sent to try to clear the enemy out of Abganerovo station, but found that the Soviets had already moved anti-tank guns into the position. However, no significant Axis forces lay between the jaws of the Soviet pincers closing on Kalach.

By the morning of 22 November, the mobile groups from Vatutin's South-Western Front were within striking range of their primary objective, Kalach, but their combat power at the front of the advance was ebbing fast. Most of the Soviet infantry and artillery were still mopping up Group Lascar or guarding the flanks of the breakthrough, leaving the tank–cavalry mobile groups without much support. Furthermore, the mobile groups had been forced to detach some of their own units to deal with various obstacles, so Rodin's 26th Tank Corps was left with only two tank brigades. On the evening of 21/22 November, Rodin assigned Podpolkovnik Georgy N. Filippov to lead a group of tanks and motorized infantrymen to seize the German bridge at Kalach as soon as possible. Although most of Rodin's corps was held up west of Kalach by a *Kampfgruppe* from 24.Panzer-Division,

Filippov was able to approach the bridge during the night by placing three captured German vehicles at the front of his column. The Germans had no significant combat units in Kalach, just a single 8.8cm Flak battery, some security troops, support personnel from 16.Panzer-Division and a Pionier School. The pontoon bridge over the Don, located at Berezovskiy north-west of Kalach, was guarded by only a single 8.8cm Flak gun and a handful of security troops. Filippov's column approached the bridge just before 0800hrs and the guards were deceived by the captured vehicles until the last moment. The 8.8cm gun managed to

About 27,000 Romanian troops fell into Soviet captivity on 22–23 November 1942 when Group Lascar surrendered. Although some units managed to escape south to the Chir River, the bulk of the Romanian Third Army was demolished in four days of heavy fighting. (Author's collection)

A Panzer III Ausf. L from 22.Panzer-Division in a reserve position prior to the start of Operation *Uranus*. Heeresgruppe B positioned the division behind the Romanian Third Army to prevent an enemy breakthrough in this sector, but with only 40 operational tanks and limited fuel, it proved unable to stop an entire Soviet tank army. (Author's collection)

destroy two Soviet T-34 tanks before it was knocked out and the bridge was captured intact. Filippov's two rifle companies and 14 remaining tanks established a hedgehog defence around the bridge and awaited relief, although he did not have radio communications with Rodin. Oberst Hans Mikosch, commander of the Pionier School in Kalach, tried to organize a counter-attack against Filippov's bridgehead with an ad hoc group, but they were repulsed three times. Filippov's tiny force held the bridgehead on its own for 11 hours, until elements of the 19th Tank Brigade arrived in late afternoon and began crossing the Don. Once Soviet armour was across in force, German resistance in Kalach quickly evaporated and the town was secured by nightfall. Further north, an advance group from Kravchenko's 4th Tank Corps also secured a small bridgehead over the Don.

While the Germans were losing Kalach, Strecker's XI.Armee-Korps was being outflanked by Pliev's 3rd Guards Cavalry Corps. On the morning of 22 November, Batov's 65th Army launched another frontal assault against Strecker's corps with four rifle divisions. For the first time, Galanin's 24th Army also joined the offensive, sending two rifle divisions against Strecker's right flank, defended by 76.Infanterie-Division. Strecker's corps was now in a vice, being squeezed from three directions and in danger of becoming isolated west of the Don. Strecker decided to withdraw both 44.Infanterie-Division and 376.Infanterie-Division 10km eastwards, which forced 14.Panzer-Division to conform. The remnants of the Romanian 1st Cavalry Division and the Voiscu detachment also retreated with XI.Armee-Korps. However, the withdrawal brought only a brief reprieve because the Soviets pursued Strecker's corps and threatened to cut it off from the rest of 6.Armee. At this point, Paulus and his chief of staff, Generalmajor Arthur Schmidt, were still in Nizhne-Chirskaya, but Hitler ordered them to fly back into the emerging pocket to join their troops. During the afternoon, Paulus established his new 6.Armee headquarters at Gumrak railway station. That evening, Paulus decided that Strecker's XI.Armee-Korps needed to evacuate its bridgehead west of the Don, although this meant conducting a risky tactical withdrawal in the face of an aggressive enemy.

Meanwhile, the protracted resistance of the encircled Group Lascar kept most of 5th Tank Army's infantry busy for several days. Lascar refused two Soviet surrender demands and his troops continued to fight. Early on 22 November, the Romanian 1st Armoured Division managed to break through the Soviet ring and move south with about 30 tanks. Lascar hoped to break out with his infantry – despite orders to stay put from von Weichs – but a Soviet attack sliced his pocket into two fragments on the evening of 22 November and Lascar was captured. Two small groups of survivors managed to break out to the south, but the remaining 27,000 Romanian troops in the pocket surrendered. The rest of Romanenko's 5th Tank Army tried to move south towards the Chir River, but was hindered by small enemy pockets of resistance. Borisov's 8th Cavalry Corps managed to surround the much-reduced 22.Panzer-Division, but the German unit kept escaping southwards. Romanenko ordered Butkov's 1st Tank Corps to pivot south-east and advance to the Chir River, but with just 24 operational tanks, Butkov found this difficult to accomplish. On the evening of 22 November, von Weichs put General der Infanterie Karl-Adolf Hollidt in charge of organizing a new Axis front along the Chir, which was asking nothing short of a miracle.

Eremenko's Stalingrad Front continued to exploit the enemy weakness in their sector on 22 November, with Tolbukhin's 57th Army forcing the German IV.Armee-Korps to refuse its flank and withdraw nearly 10km back to a new line anchored on Tsybenko. Despite fuel resupply issues, Volskiy's 4th Mechanized Corps continued pushing west 35km against light resistance and reached its objective, the Sovetskiy State Farm, by 1220hrs. At this point, only 14km separated the vanguards of the Stalingrad Front from those of the South-Western Front. Another column from Volskiy's corps pushed north to Karpovka, the site of 6.Armee's forward supply base. Along the way, the Soviets overran a major fuel dump in Novyi Put. However, Paulus had decided to send forces to this sector to build a new front between Marinovka-Karpovka and along the Chervlenaya River, facing south-west. Kampfgruppe von Hanstein (a mixed force from 3.Infanterie-Division and 60.Infanterie-Division) arrived at Karpovka just ahead of the Soviets, with

German reconnaissance units were often forced to conduct mobile delaying operations to hinder Soviet breaches in the front line. Here, an SdKfz 222 (right) and an SdKfz 232 8-rad (left) armoured car are positioned near a Russian village. Both vehicles are equipped with 2cm cannons, which enable them to engage enemy infantry and light vehicles. German delaying tactics could hinder Operation *Uranus*, but not stop it. (From the fonds of the RGAKFD in Krasnogorsk via Stavka)

11 tanks and a battalion of infantry. One of Volskiy's mechanized brigades attacked Karpovka station, but was stopped by stiff resistance. In the south, Shapkin's 4th Cavalry Corps continued to push back the thin Romanian screen and would capture Aksai the next day.

The Soviets moved to conclude Operation *Uranus* on 23 November, but began to shift focus towards follow-on missions. In particular, Tolbukhin's 57th Army became focused on breaking through the thin German defensive line erected around Karpovka, which resulted in an extended fight for this position. Tanaschishin's 13th Tank Corps was committed to an unsuccessful frontal assault against the German IV.Armee-Korps, while part of Volskiy's 4th Mechanized Corps and the 15th Guards Rifle Division tried and failed to capture Karpovka. German reinforcements poured into this critical sector, including Marder II tank destroyers and more tanks. A counter-attack by Leyser's 29.Infanterie-Division (mot.) pushed the Soviets back and inflicted painful losses. The rest of Volskiy's 4th Mechanized Corps was hampered by ammunition and fuel shortages, preventing it from moving much this day. Around 1600hrs, a column of tanks was seen approaching the Sovetskiy State Farm No. 2, where Polkovnik Mikhail I. Rodionov's 36th Mechanized Brigade was located. According to the plan, Soviet forces from the South-Western Front were supposed to fire green flares when they encountered troops of the Stalingrad Front, but this did not occur. Consequently, Rodionov's troops thought the approaching tanks were German vehicles and opened fire. In fact, these were Podpolkovnik Pyotr K. Zhidrov's T-34 tanks from the 45th Tank Brigade in Kravchenko's 4th Tank Corps. Both Soviet units fired on each other, inflicting some casualties. Soviet propaganda was quick to erase this embarrassing friendly fire incident from the history of the event, which was recorded for posterity as a joyous link up between troops of the two fronts. However, the important point was that 6.Armee was now encircled in and around Stalingrad – the first time this had ever happened to a complete German army. Although over 30,000 Axis troops managed to escape southwards before the jaws of the Soviet pincers closed, about 284,000 remained trapped in the Stalingrad pocket. Despite supply problems and unexpected enemy resistance, Operation *Uranus* had produced an unqualified operational success for the Red Army.

THE INITIAL GERMAN REACTION, 24–28 NOVEMBER 1942

Once it was clear the Axis forces in Stalingrad were encircled, everyone assumed that Hitler would order 6.Armee to conduct a breakout operation. The Soviet Stavka and front commanders expected it and began to redeploy their forces to contain a breakout. Paulus and von Weichs also expected it and directed their staffs to begin planning for a breakout operation. However, Hitler had no intention of retreating from Stalingrad, because he felt this would be regarded as a major defeat. From the start of the Stalingrad crisis, Hitler grasped for any straw, any miracle, which might avoid a humiliating defeat. While still at Berchtesgaden on 20 November, Hitler asked Generaloberst Hans Jeschonnek, Luftwaffe chief of staff, if the Luftwaffe could supply 6.Armee by air. Without putting any real thought into the matter, Jeschonnek thought an airlift was suitable and pointed out

that the Luftwaffe had successfully supplied the encircled II.Armee-Korps at Demyansk in February–May 1942. Two days later, Reichsmarschall Hermann Göring arrived at Berchtesgaden and confirmed that his Luftwaffe could supply 6.Armee by air; indeed, he promised the delivery of 500 tons per day. Buoyed by these assurances – but without consulting actual technical experts or commanders in the field – Hitler convinced himself that an airlift would enable 6.Armee to survive until von Manstein's relief effort began. Generalleutnant Martin Fiebig, commander of VIII.Fliegerkorps, had already told Paulus on 21 November that the Luftwaffe did not have enough aircraft to supply 6.Armee by air. Unaware of Hitler's reasoning, at 2345hrs on 23 November, Paulus sent a radio signal to the OKW, requesting 'freedom of action', which meant permission to conduct a breakout. The next morning, Hitler sent a signal to Paulus, informing him that 6.Armee was to hold its position and would be supplied by air, until von Manstein restored ground communications.

Early on, most of the Luftwaffe commanders realized that supplying 6.Armee by air was not really feasible. Jeschonnek's comparison with the Demyansk airlift was specious, because in that case the Luftwaffe had only supported six encircled divisions (96,000 troops) with a daily average of 300 tons for three months. On the best day of the Demyansk airlift, the Luftwaffe delivered 544 tons of supplies. Furthermore, the Demyansk airlift was costly, resulting in the loss of 106 Ju 52 transports. In the current situation, 6.Armee was a much larger force and the Luftwaffe thought it would require at least 750 tons of supplies per day. In fact, the 6.Armee quartermasters knew that even 750 tons per day would not be sufficient to keep the army combat-capable for very long. Given the limited transport units in theatre, the distance involved and poor flying weather, the Luftwaffe would be hard-pressed to deliver even a fraction of the daily requirements. When Hitler ordered the airlift to begin, Fiebig only had 25 operational Ju 52 transports on hand, each capable of lifting 2 tons of supplies. Nearly one-third of the Luftwaffe's transport force was already engaged in supporting the air bridge to Tunisia, meaning that the only reserves of pilots and aircraft were in the flight schools in Germany. Nevertheless, the Luftwaffe obediently set about trying to accomplish the impossible. Fiebig made his headquarters at Tatsinskaya airfield, which was located 237km from Gumrak airfield in the pocket. Morozovskaya airfield, 194km from Gumrak, was also used in the airlift. In order to boost Fiebig's airlift capability, the Oberkommando der

Desperate for transport aircraft, the Luftwaffe pressed two squadrons of obsolete Ju 86 bombers into service during the Stalingrad airlift. Out of a total of 58 Ju 86 taken from training units in Germany, 42 were lost during the airlift. (Süddeutsche Zeitung, Bild 00384768, Foto: Scherl)

The Don Front positioned 12 anti-aircraft regiments around the Stalingrad pocket, with nearly 200 85mm guns, forcing low-flying Luftwaffe transports to run the gauntlet. Here a battery of 85mm guns (52-K) wait for the Luftwaffe to appear. The Soviet air defence lacked radar warning and often did not see enemy aircraft until they were very close. (Nik Cornish at www.Stavka.org.uk)

Luftwaffe (OKL) began transferring five transport groups to the region, with about 150 aircraft. In extremis, the Luftwaffe also decided to use He 111, He 177 and Fw 200 bombers to deliver supplies. However, when the airlift began on 24 November, the Luftwaffe managed to deliver just 86 tons on the first day and a total of only 269 tons during the first five days of the airlift. Since 6.Armee's food reserves were still assessed as adequate, the airlift at first prioritized fuel and ammunition.

In the early days of the encirclement, the supply situation in 6.Armee was serious but not immediately dangerous. The army had about 12 days of rations on hand. Typically, German soldiers received about 1,300–1,500g of food per day, including 750g of bread and 260g of meat. Once the encirclement began, rations were reduced to 400g of bread and 120g of meat. The 6.Armee tried to preserve its 25,000 horses for as long as possible since they were needed to move artillery around the perimeter, but without fodder they would not last long and all were destined to be converted into horsemeat for consumption. Ammunition stocks were low, particularly for artillery and anti-tank units, which meant that German defensive firepower had to be carefully rationed. Fuel quickly became a rare commodity, with just enough to move mission-critical vehicles.

Since he was not authorized to break out, Paulus was forced to reconfigure his forces for an extended siege. Yet before Paulus could even issue any new command guidance, General der Artillerie Walter von Seydlitz-Kurzbach, commander of LI.Armee-Korps, tried to force his hand. Seydlitz had led the operation that relieved the Demyansk pocket six months earlier and he favoured decisive action, rather than awaiting relief. On his own initiative, Seydlitz issued Korpsbefehl (Corps Order) No. 118 at 2240hrs on 23 November; it instructed units to prepare for a breakout. As part of the order, Seydlitz directed 3.Infanterie-Division (mot.) and 94.Infanterie-Division to evacuate their positions in the north-east corner of the pocket and fall back 4km in anticipation of a breakout attempt. The Soviet 66th Army noticed the withdrawal and attacked the 94.Infanterie-Division with tanks and infantry, inflicting over 200 casualties. Although Hitler was angered when he heard about the unauthorized withdrawal, there were no repercussions. Paulus also tolerated this act of insubordination, demonstrating his own leadership shortcomings. In terms of dispositions, Paulus' main concern was to evacuate XI.Armee-Korps from the west side of the Don River and to establish a strong defensive perimeter around Gumrak airfield. Hube's XIV.Panzer-Korps would hold the south-western side of the pocket, while Jaenecke's IV.Armee-Korps would anchor the south-east corner of the pocket.

Once 6.Armee was encircled, Rokossovsky's Don Front focused on destroying the three infantry divisions (44., 376. and 384.) of Strecker's XI.Armee-Korps, which was vulnerable in the Sirotinskaya bridgehead west of the Don. While Batov's 65th Army conducted frontal assaults against Strecker's centre beginning on 25 November, Galanin's 24th Army attacked his right flank. Pliev's 3rd Guards Cavalry Corps tried to get around

The Yak-1 fighter was the primary interceptor used by the Soviet 8th and 16th Air armies around Stalingrad in late 1942. Soviet fighters proved adept at shooting down the slow-moving enemy transport planes flying in and out of Stalingrad, despite the best efforts of the Luftwaffe fighter escorts. (Author's collection)

Strecker's left flank, but was stopped by *Kampfgruppen* from 16.Panzer-Division and 24.Panzer-Division. The Germans conducted a slow, fighting withdrawal to the Don, inflicting considerable losses on the pursuing Soviet troops. In particular, the 3rd Guards Cavalry Corps suffered over 40 per cent losses. Although hard-pressed, the last of Strecker's units succeeded in crossing the frozen Don on the night of 26/27 November, then blew up the pontoon bridge at Vertyachii at 0340hrs on 27 November. After evacuating the Sirotinskaya bridgehead, Paulus transferred 16.Panzer-Division and 24.Panzer-Division from the west side of the pocket to the north-east corner, where they were assigned to LI.Armee-Korps. Icy roads and fuel shortages made this transfer difficult and it was the last major redistribution of forces within the pocket.

Von Manstein and his staff arrived at Novocherkassk near Rostov on the morning of 26 November and issued an order activating Heeresgruppe Don. Yet aside from the encircled 6.Armee in Stalingrad, von Manstein initially had very few troops available. Hollidt's own XVII.Armee-Korps anchored the left flank of Heeresgruppe Don with two German infantry divisions (62. and 294.) and two Romanian infantry divisions (7th and 11th). On the morning of 25 November, the two German divisions conducted a successful spoiling attack against Lelyushenko's 1st Guards Army, which routed two Soviet divisions. Thus far, Lelyushenko's army had only served as a flank guard for 5th Tank Army. Further south, the battered remnants of 22.Panzer-Division and the Romanian 1st Armoured Division (28 tanks) linked up with the German 403.Sicherungs-Division and formed a defensive line behind the northern arm of the Chir River. Although XXXXVIII.Panzer-Korps had inflicted considerable delay upon Romanenko's 5th Tank Army, Hitler was infuriated that the mobile reserve had failed to defeat the enemy breakthrough and ordered Heim placed under arrest on 26 November. Some remnants of the Romanian Third Army managed to escape encirclement, but the only unit to reach the Chir intact was Major Gheorghe Rasconescu's 1st Battalion, 15th Infantry Regiment (6th Infantry Division); the battalion marched 140km over the course of three nights, moving on foot over the icy steppe, until reaching friendly forces on the Chir. In recognition of his feat, the Germans awarded Rasconescu the Ritterkreuz des Eisernen

A crashed Ju 52 transport plane. The Ju 52 was the Luftwaffe's primary workhorse during the airlift, able to deliver just over 2 tons in one sortie. However, a total of 260 Ju 62s were lost during the airlift, representing roughly one-third of the Luftwaffe's transport force. (Nik Cornish at www. Stavka.org.uk)

Kreuzes. Dumitrescu moved his Third Army headquarters to Morozovskaya, but all the remaining Romanian troops were placed under Hollidt's command.

The most vulnerable area that Hollidt had to defend was along the main Rostov–Stalingrad rail line, particularly in the sector between Oblivskaya airfield (headquarters of VIII.Fliegerkorps) and Nizhne-Chirskaya. By chance, Panzer-Kompanie Abendroth arrived at Oblivskaya with 11 Panzer III Ausf. J tanks on 26 November, but Hollidt had no large combat units to defend this vital sector, just a collection of alarm units and *Kampfgruppen* made from Luftwaffe personnel and support troops. For example, Kampfgruppe Tschücke, defending the area east of the vital Chir railway station, was formed around three companies from Pionier-Bataillon 672 and rounded out with about 150 support troops that escaped from the pocket; the group's heavy weapons consisted of one 8.8cm Flak gun, two 7.5cm anti-tank guns and one 2cm quad Flak gun. Kampfgruppe Stumpfeld, defending Surovikino, was built around the staff of Arko 108 and the Estonian 36th Defence Battalion. The heterogeneous collection of Axis units hastily cobbled together to defend the Chir were poorly armed and equipped, but Romanenko's 5th Tank Army moved slowly towards the Chir and frittered away much of its combat power before reaching its final objectives. Romanenko sent only a single small unit, the 8th Motorcycle Regiment, ahead to seize Oblivskaya airbase and block the rail line, but it failed to accomplish this task. Before Romanenko recognized his mistake, Rasconescu's battalion was sent to defend Oblivskaya airbase and Heeresgruppe B began transferring reinforcements to this sector. Von Weichs decided to strip the few German units supporting the Italian and Hungarian armies and send them to Hollidt. By 28 November, the first three battalions from 336.Infanterie-Division had arrived from Heeresgruppe B.

Hitler promised von Manstein two Panzer, four infantry and one Luftwaffe division as reinforcements, but was vague about when they would arrive and in what condition. The most formidable reinforcement was Generalmajor Erhard Raus' full-strength 6.Panzer-Division, just beginning to arrive from France; this unit had 150 tanks. Generalmajor Hermann Balck's 11.Panzer-Division was being transferred from Heeresgruppe Mitte, but this division had only 70 tanks, and the 17.Panzer-Division, which was also earmarked for Heeresgruppe Don, had just 57 tanks. Heeresgruppe A in the Caucasus was supposed to transfer 23.Panzer-Division to support Hoth's forces around Kotelnikovo, but it was delayed by transport difficulties. A handful of infantry divisions were en route to von Manstein, such as 306.Infanterie-Division from Belgium, but these units arrived in bits and pieces. While Hollidt was trying to organize a defence on the Chir River, Hoth reformed the remnants of the Romanian Fourth Army into a screening force to protect the rail line north to Stalingrad from Kotelnikovo. At best, the Romanian 18th Infantry Division, the 5th and 8th Cavalry divisions and survivors from the VI Corps might have been capable of preventing the Soviet 4th Cavalry Corps from pushing south of the Aksai River, but could not stop a serious advance by the 51st Army with tanks and infantry.

Although the Red Army had achieved a great victory with Operation *Uranus*, its leaders made some poor operational choices in the immediate aftermath of the encirclement; these poor choices were influenced by the lack of hard intelligence about enemy reserves. Instead of focusing on trying to prevent the Axis from forming a new line on the Chir River, the South-Western, Don and Stalingrad fronts committed their best units to try to reduce 6.Armee's perimeter. Vasilevskiy and Stavka were concerned that 6.Armee might either break out of the pocket or the Germans might mount a successful relief effort, so reduction of the Stalingrad pocket became the priority. Vatutin was ordered to transfer Chistiakov's 21st Army to Rokossovsky's Don Front, which seriously reduced the forces heading towards the Chir River. Instead, the primary mobile units – the 4th Mechanized Corps, 4th and 26th Tank Corps and 3rd Guards Cavalry Corps – were committed against the west side of the pocket, but without adequate artillery or infantry support. Not only did 6.Armee have some of its best units in the Marinovka sector, but they even managed to lay some mines and obstacles. Consequently, the Soviet cavalry and mechanized units suffered heavy losses. By 28 November, Kravchenko's 4th Tank Corps was reduced to 27 tanks and Rodin's 26th Tank Corps had just 25 tanks. Romanenko's 5th Tank Army, which was assigned to bounce the Chir River, had also lost most of its armour and Butkov's 1st Tank Corps was placed in reserve. By the time that Romanenko's army reached the Chir River, its strength was ebbing and it had to rely primarily upon infantry units to try to break the Axis line.

German soldiers use a horse-drawn sled to move supplies from the airfield to army supply units around the perimeter. Needless to say, a rudimentary logistic system such as this could not sustain a modern military force for very long. Once the fuel was gone and the horses were eaten, 6.Armee's logistic system collapsed. (Nik Cornish at www.Stavka.org.uk)

The lucky ones. The Luftwaffe was able to fly out over 24,000 wounded personnel from 6.Armee during the airlift, but roughly 40,000 wounded remained in the pocket to the end. (Süddeutsche Zeitung, Bild 02906432)

AIR BLOCKADE, 0830HRS, 11 DECEMBER 1942 (PP. 48–49)

By the time that VIII.Fliegerkorps had managed to get enough aircraft and pilots to mount a large-scale airlift operation to the encircled 6.Armee at Stalingrad, the Soviet VVS had taken measures to thwart that operation. General-polkovnik Aleksandr A. Novikov, commander-in-chief of the Soviet Air Forces, ordered the 8th Air Army and 16th Air Army to establish air blockade zones around Stalingrad in order to intercept incoming German transport aircraft. Although the VVS did not have RUS-2 radars in the Stalingrad sectors, both air armies maintained continuous air patrols along the likely German air corridors into the pocket. The Red Army also emplaced numerous anti-aircraft units in a 5km-wide ring around the perimeter of the Stalingrad pocket. The Luftwaffe only had one fighter unit, a detachment with about three to six operational Bf 109Gs from I./Jagdgeschwader 3 stationed at Pitomnik airfield, to provide escort for transport sorties into the pocket, whereas the two Soviet air armies had over 200 fighters to use in the air blockade. German fighters based at Morozovskaya airfield were not provided with long-range fuel tanks until late January 1943. Consequently, the Luftwaffe tried to sneak its Ju 52 transports into Pitomnik airfield during periods of bad weather and poor visibility. By flying low, in small groups, the Ju 52s were difficult for Soviet fighters to spot, although losses due to flight accidents mounted.

By 7 December, VIII.Fliegerkorps managed to fly over 300 tons of supplies into the Stalingrad pocket; this was still well short of the army's logistic requirements, but a significant improvement over the early days of the airlift. However, the VVS was also honing its ability to detect and destroy incoming transports, and on 11 December they unleashed two veteran fighter regiments: the 3rd Guards Fighter Regiment equipped with La-5 fighters, and the 9th Guards Fighter Regiment equipped with Yak-1 fighters. The Luftwaffe attempted to fly 117 transports and bombers to Pitomnik over the course of the day, but with only a handful of escorts, including one Italian C.202 fighter. The German transports flew in groups of three, usually just a few hundred metres above the ground. Given better than usual visibility conditions, the Soviet fighter pilots were able to spot the lumbering German transports and attack them. The handful of escort fighters could do little to protect the spread-out clusters of transports.

Here, Leytenant Petr V. Bazanov (**1**), from 3rd Guards Fighter Regiment, shoots down a Ju 52 transport (**2**) about 10km south-west of Pitomnik. The transport's wing is already coming off, in flames. Bazanov would bag another Ju 52 shortly afterwards. Another Soviet La-5 (**3**) is also shooting at one of the other Ju 52s in the same group. In total, Soviet fighters and anti-aircraft destroyed a total of 14 Luftwaffe transports on 11 December. Although the Luftwaffe lacked the resources to fully supply the trapped 6.Armee by air, Novikov's air blockade made the airlift fail more quickly and at greater cost.

THE BATTLE OF THE CHIR RIVER, 30 NOVEMBER–15 DECEMBER 1942

By 28 November, the western edge of the Stalingrad pocket was 50km from the nearest positions of Armee-Abteilung Hollidt at Rychovskiy. Gruppe Hoth's forces at Kotelnikovo were about 140km from the southern edge of the Stalingrad pocket. If von Manstein was going to organize a successful relief operation of 6.Armee, retaining the logistic bases along the Chir River was a vital prerequisite. On the other side of the hill, the Soviets did not fully recognize the importance of destroying Group Hollidt until the end of November. Even then, Vatutin struggled to mass combat power on the Chir River. Indeed, Romanenko's 5th Tank Army was already five days behind schedule and the Germans were beginning to recover from the shock of Operation *Uranus*. Vatutin did manage to retrieve four rifle divisions and Pliev's 3rd Guards Cavalry Corps from the Don Front to re-energize the push towardd the Chir, as well as over 100 new tanks to rebuild Butkov's 1st Tank Corps. Romanenko was ordered to capture the enemy strongpoints at Oblivskaya, Surovikino and Rychovskiy as soon as possible. Although Romanenko had four cavalry and five rifle divisions near the Chir, he had very little artillery and tank support. On 28–30 November, Romanenko's 5th Tank Army launched a series of uncoordinated attacks against multiple points along the Chir front, but failed to achieve any success because his forces were dispersed rather than concentrated. Pliev's 3rd Guards Cavalry Corps attacked Kampfgruppe Tschücke at Rychovskiy on 29 November, but was repulsed with heavy losses. Five Soviet tanks supported the attack, but were picked off by 8.8cm Flak guns and *Pioniere* wielding Hafthohlladung hollow-charge mines. Pliev attacked again the next day and was beaten back. Borisov's 8th Cavalry Corps attacked the Estonians and Luftwaffe troops holding Oblivskaya and was bloodily repulsed. Due to improving weather, VIII.Fliegerkorps was able to provide effective close air support sorties, which inflicted heavy losses on the Soviet units attacking Oblivskaya airfield. Oberleutnant Hans-Ulrich Rudel claimed to have flown no fewer than 17 sorties on one day, against enemy units that were only a short distance from the airfield. Although the VVS also became more active in the skies, it did

A pair of Soviet BA 10M armoured cars with tracks advance to complete the encirclement of 6.Armee. The 4th Mechanized Corps had an organic armoured car battalion with 20 BA-10 armoured cars, which had a good mix of mobility and firepower in snow and ice. (Nik Cornish at www. Stavka.org.uk)

Battle of the Chir River, 30 November–15 December 1942

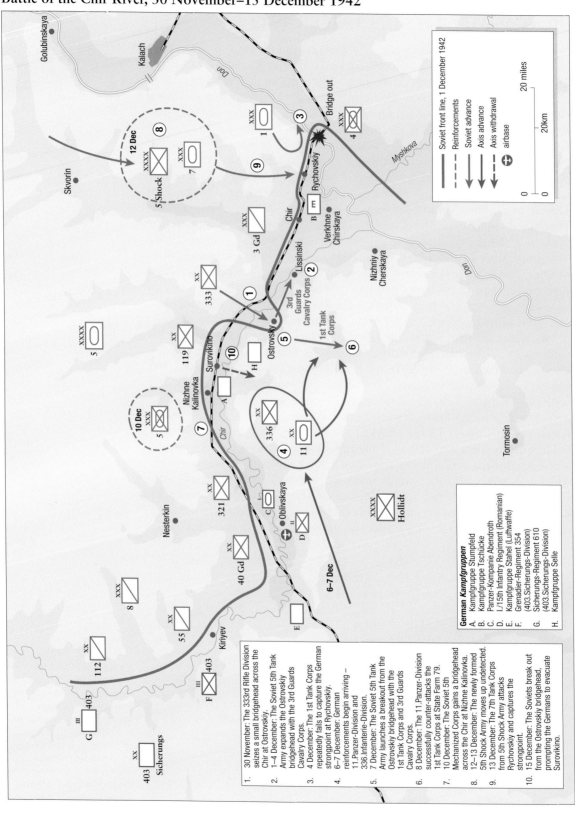

Golubinskaya
Kalach
Don
Skvorin
12 Dec
8
XXXX
XXX
7
5 Shock
XXX
1
3
Bridge out
XXX
4
Rychovskiy
Myshkova
9
XXX
3 Gd
Chir
Lissinski
2
Verkhne Chirskaya
B
3rd Guards Cavalry Corps
XX
333
1
Ostrovskiy
5
Nizhniy Cherskaya
1st Tank Corps
6
XX
119
Surovikino
10
H
A
Nizhne Kalinovka
7
10 Dec
XXX
5
XX
336
11
4
XX
Don
Tormosin
XXXX
5
XX
321
Oblivskaya
C
D
XXXX
Hollidt
Nesterkin
6–7 Dec
XX
40 Gd
E
Kiriyev
XXX
8
XX
55
XX
403
XX
112
III
403
F
III
403
G
XX
403
Sicherungs

German Kampfgruppen
A. Kampfgruppe Stumpfeld
B. Kampfgruppe Tschucke
C. Panzer-Kompanie Abendroth
D. I/15th Infantry Regiment (Romanian)
E. Kampfgruppe Stahel (Luftwaffe)
F. Grenadier-Regiment 354 (403.Sicherungs-Division)
G. Sicherungs-Regiment 610 (403.Sicherungs-Division)
H. Kampfgruppe Selle

Soviet front line, 1 December 1942
Reinforcements
Soviet advance
Axis advance
Axis withdrawal
airbase

0   20km
0   20 miles

1. 30 November: The 333rd Rifle Division seizes a small bridgehead across the Chir at Ostrovskiy.
2. 1–4 December: The Soviet 5th Tank Army expands the Ostrovskiy bridgehead with the 3rd Guards Cavalry Corps.
3. 4 December: The 1st Tank Corps repeatedly fails to capture the German strongpoint at Rychovskiy.
4. 6–7 December: German reinforcements begin arriving – 11.Panzer-Division and 336.Infanterie-Division.
5. 7 December: The Soviet 5th Tank Army launches a breakout from the Ostrovskiy bridgehead with the 1st Tank Corps and 3rd Guards Cavalry Corps.
6. 8 December: The 11.Panzer-Division successfully counter-attacks the 1st Tank Corps at State Farm 79.
7. 10 December: The Soviet 5th Mechanized Corps gains a bridgehead across the Chir at Nizhne Kalinovka.
8. 12–13 December: The newly formed 5th Shock Army moves up undetected.
9. 13 December: The 7th Tank Corps from 5th Shock Army attacks Rychovskiy and captures the strongpoint.
10. 15 December: The Soviets break out from the Ostrovskiy bridgehead, prompting the Germans to evacuate Surovikino.

52

not appear much over the Chir battlefield, leaving the Luftwaffe with local air superiority in this sector. Elsewhere, two Soviet rifle divisions tried to cross the upper Chir near Chernyshevskaya, but were stymied by XXXXVIII. Panzer-Korps, which put in an exemplary performance. The only place where Romanenko's 5th Tank Army achieved any real success was 10km south-east of Surovikino, where the 333rd Rifle Division managed to gain a bridgehead across the Chir at Ostrovskiy on the morning of 30 November and partly surrounded Kampfgruppe Korntner (an 850-man alarm unit). However, before Romanenko could exploit the success, Kampfgruppe Selle arrived to block the Soviet infantrymen and rescue the isolated German troops. Amazingly, the ad hoc Axis units succeeded in fending off multiple attacks by the 5th Tank Army and prevented them from getting across the Chir in force.

While Romanenko was failing to accomplish his mission on the Chir, the Don Front and part of the Stalingrad Front continued to execute Vasilevskiy's strategy of trying to reduce the Stalingrad pocket as quickly as possible. Since Hitler had declared Stalingrad to be a fortress, Paulus set about establishing a strong defensive perimeter, which meant pulling XI.Armee-Korps back from the Don. The 21st and 65th armies were able to advance several kilometres across the frozen steppe until they ran into the new German main line of resistance, which was shorter and easier to defend. By this point, the Soviet front-line units had lost a good deal of their combat effectiveness and could not break prepared German defences. The 66th Army also attacked the north-east corner of the pocket, but its one small penetration was quickly eliminated. With a smaller perimeter, Paulus was able to create a mobile reserve from 14.Panzer-Division, which he dispatched to sectors under attack. Thereafter, operations around the perimeter of the Stalingrad pocket settled into positional warfare, with the front barely moving for the next six weeks. One bright spot for the Soviets was that VVS fighters were able to inflict significant losses on the Luftwaffe units involved in the Stalingrad airlift, shooting down 13 Ju 52 transports between 28 and 30 November. Eremenko's Stalingrad Front also continued to attack the southern side of the pocket with the 57th and 64th armies, but failed to achieve any real success. The front's primary mobile groups from the 4th Mechanized Corps and 13th Tank Corps remained locked in pointless combat around Karpovka station with Hube's XIV.Panzer-Korps, which still had a large number of operational panzers. Only Trufanov's 51st Army continued to push south against Hoth's forces, with two cavalry and three rifle divisions against about 6,000 Romanian survivors from the VI Corps and Kampfgruppe von Pannwitz (a mixed group that had 18 tanks and eight assault guns, but very little infantry). However, Trufanov was aware that German reinforcements were arriving at Kotelnikovo station, and by 30 November he ordered his small command to shift to the defence.

After the initial failed effort to break Hollidt's line on the Chir, Stavka decided to reinforce Romanenko's 5th Tank Army and prepare for a set-piece offensive. General Mikhail V. Volkov's 5th Mechanized Corps with 200 tanks (mostly British-built Matildas and Valentines) was transferred to Romanenko's command, along with the 8th Guards Tank Brigade (38 KV-1 heavy tanks) and additional artillery assets. Until these forces arrived, Romanenko continued regular attacks on the German strongpoints along the Chir, which continued to hold out. Stukas from VIII.Fliegerkorps were used to break up Soviet daylight attacks, with little interference from the VVS. However, Hollidt could not stop

The Soviet 5th Mechanized Corps that fought on the Chir River was mostly equipped with British-made Matilda (Mk II) and Valentine (Mk III) tanks. Here, a forlorn Valentine lies in the snow, apparently knocked out by enemy anti-tank fire. Slow-moving tanks like the Valentine were particularly vulnerable to anti-tank fire on the open steppe. (Nik Cornish at www.Stavka.org.uk)

Romanenko from reinforcing and expanding the Ostrovskiy bridgehead with Butkov's refitted 1st Tank Corps. Vatutin planned to launch a major breakout from the bridgehead on 7 December, in conjunction with a renewed attack to seize Surovikino. Just prior to the Soviet offensive on the Chir, Generalmajor Otto von Knobelsdorff took command of XXXXVIII.Panzer-Korps and both Balck's 11.Panzer-Division and the rest of 336.Infanterie-Division arrived at Morozovskaya. Elements of 7.Luftwaffen-Feld-Division were also arriving to reinforce the defence of Surovikino.

Romanenko began his breakout offensive at 0900hrs on 7 December, using the 333rd Rifle Division to penetrate the German lines, then Butkov's 1st Tank Corps pushed through in brigade columns. A regiment from 7.Luftwaffen-Feld-Division was overrun and Butkov's tanks pushed south 6km to seize Sovkhoz (State Farm) 79 by 1030hrs. Amazingly, Butkov then shifted to the tactical defence around the farm. Given the weakness of his forces, von Knobelsdorff decided to conduct a very active defence. Before Pliev's 3rd Guards Cavalry Corps could mount its supporting attack from the eastern side of the bridgehead, the Germans launched a spoiling attack with a regiment of 336.Infanterie-Division and Abendroth's tanks, which sent the Soviet cavalrymen tumbling backwards. Balck moved 11.Panzer-Division north to meet Butkov's 1st Tank Corps and managed to approach undetected from the west during the night of 7/8 December. At 0650hrs on 8 December, Balck launched a sudden attack with his division, which not only caught Butkov by surprise, but also managed to temporarily surround most of the Soviet tank corps. In the Battle of Sovkhoz 79, the Soviet tankers finally managed to fight their way out of encirclement but lost over 50 tanks in the process. Balk had mauled the Soviet armoured spearhead with a well-timed counter-stroke.

On the morning of 9 December, Volkov's 5th Mechanized Corps tried to get across the Chir west of Surovikino, but failed. A second attempt the next day succeeded in gaining a small bridgehead at Nizhne Kalinovka. Von Knobelsdorff ignored the second Soviet bridgehead and instead ordered Balck's 11.Panzer-Division to concentrate on smashing Butkov's 1st Tank Corps in the Ostrovskiy bridgehead. Although Balck achieved some success, Pliev's 3rd Guards Cavalry Corps seized another bridgehead across the Chir at Lissinski, further complicating matters. Confronting three separate Soviet bridgeheads, Balck was forced to split 11.Panzer-Division, sending part to crush the Lissinski bridgehead on 12 December and another group to block the 5th Mechanized Corps. Unknown to von Knobelsdorff, Stavka had been alarmed by the defeat of Butkov's 1st Tank Corps and decided to commit strong additional reinforcements to the fighting on the Chir. A new formation, the 5th Shock Army, was created under General-leytenant Markian M. Popov, incorporating units from the

Von Manstein employed 11.Panzer-Division as a fire brigade on the Chir, using it to fend off Soviet efforts to get across the river. Although greatly outnumbered, small German mechanized *Kampfgruppen* demonstrated great tactical ability in preventing the Red Army from immediately exploiting south towards Rostov. (Süddeutsche Zeitung, Bild 00398675, Foto: Scherl)

Stalingrad Front reserves and the RVGK. In particular, Popov was provided with the fresh 7th and 23rd Tank corps, plus the 4th Mechanized Corps and five rifle divisions. Stavka gave Popov just four days to prepare his forces to attack on the Chir. During the night of 12/13 December, Popov's army moved into their attack positions, without being detected by the Germans.

On the morning of 13 December, Popov's 5th Shock Army attacked the German strongpoint at Rychovskiy with General-mayor Pavel A. Rotmistrov's 7th Tank Corps and two rifle divisions (4th Guards Rifle Division, 258th Rifle Division). After a 30-minute preparation by mortars and Katyusha rockets, Rotmistrov's mass of armour pushed into the village and German resistance quickly collapsed. The Red Army used a sledgehammer to smash a walnut. Those members of the garrison not killed in the assault fled south, towards Verkhne-Chirskii. Rotmistrov's tankers attacked that German strongpoint the next morning, but were repulsed with the loss of about 20 tanks. Rotmistrov decided to follow up with a night attack, which successfully captured Verkhne-Chirskii during the night of 14/15 December. Meanwhile, Butkov's remaining tanks broke out of the Ostrovskiy bridgehead, while Volkov's 5th Mechanized Corps expanded its bridgehead at Nizhne Kalinovka. Von Knobelsdorff's forces were stretched to breaking point, and he was forced to evacuate Surovikino. At this point, Stavka was satisfied that XXXXVIII.Panzer-Korps was in no position to mount a relief operation from the Chir River, and it opted to reduce the tempo of fighting in this sector because Vatutin's South-Western Front was about to commence Operation *Little Saturn* against the Italian Eighth Army.

WINTERGEWITTER, 12–29 DECEMBER 1942

It did not take long for von Manstein's well-trained staff at Heeresgruppe Don to develop a plan, designated as *Wintergewitter* (*Winter Storm*), to re-establish ground communications with the encircled 6.Armee. The basic plan was envisioned as a classic pincer operation with XXXXVIII.Panzer-Korps attacking north-east from the Chir River and LVII.Panzer-Korps pushing north from Kotelnikovo. Although assessed as very high risk, the plan appeared feasible in early December, but success was dependent on two key

Operation *Wintergewitter (Winter Storm)*, 12–29 December 1942

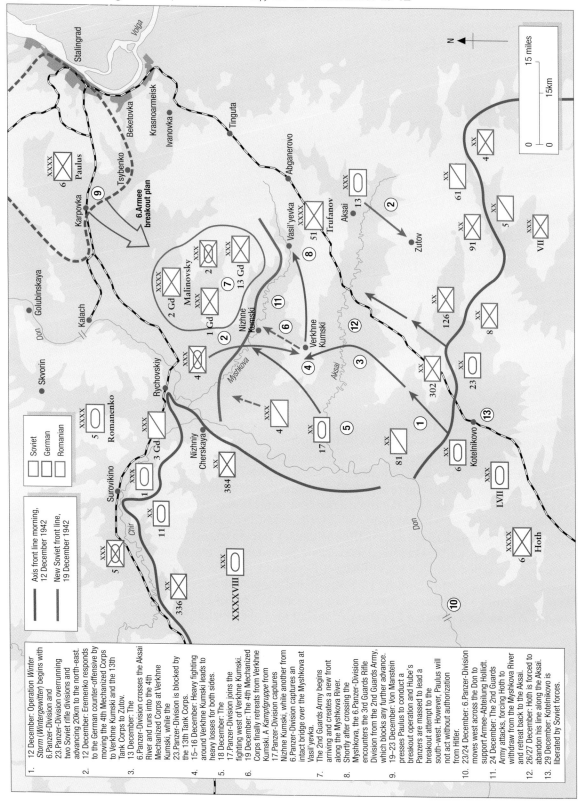

1. 12 December: Operation *Winter Storm (Wintergewitter)* begins with 6.Panzer-Division and 23.Panzer-Division overrunning two Soviet rifle divisions and advancing 20km to the north-east.

2. 12 December: Eremenko responds to the German counter-offensive by moving the 4th Mechanized Corps to Verkhne Kumski and the 13th Tank Corps to Zutov.

3. 13 December: The 6.Panzer-Division crosses the Aksai River and runs into the 4th Mechanized Corps at Verkhne Kumski, while the 23.Panzer-Division is blocked by the 13th Tank Corps.

4. 15–16 December: Heavy fighting around Verkhne Kumski leads to heavy losses for both sides.

5. 18 December: The 17.Panzer-Division joins the fighting west of Verkhne Kumski.

6. 19 December: The 4th Mechanized Corps finally retreats from Verkhne Kumski. A *Kampfgruppe* from 17.Panzer-Division captures Nizhne Kumski, while another from 6.Panzer-Division captures an intact bridge over the Myshkova at Vasil'yevka.

7. The 2nd Guards Army begins arriving and creates a new front along the Myshkova River.

8. Shortly after crossing the Myshkova, the 6.Panzer-Division encounters the 3rd Guards Rifle Division from the 2nd Guards Army, which blocks any further advance.

9. 19–23 December: Von Manstein presses Paulus to conduct a breakout operation and Hube's Panzers are massed to lead a breakout attempt to the south-west. However, Paulus will not act without authorization from Hitler.

10. 23/24 December: 6.Panzer-Division moves west across the Don to support Armee-Abteilung Hollidt.

11. 24 December: The 2nd Guards Army attacks, forcing Hoth to withdraw from the Myshkova River and retreat back to the Aksai.

12. 26/27 December: Hoth is forced to abandon his line along the Aksai.

13. 29 December: Kotelnikovo is liberated by Soviet forces.

assumptions: first, that the requisite *Panzer-Divisionen* could be assembled quickly and second, that the Red Army would not pull any more major operational surprises. Both planning assumptions proved false. By 10 December, it was clear that XXXXVIII. Panzer-Korps was fighting for its life on the Chir River and would not be able to participate in *Wintergewitter*. Instead, von Manstein was forced to modify the relief operation into a single thrust by Hoth's forces, which were smaller than expected. Despite its title, Armeegruppe Hoth consisted of only General der Panzertruppe Friedrich Kirchner's LVII.Panzer-Korps

Hoth kicked off *Wintergewitter* on 12 December 1942 and made excellent progress on the first day of the operation, scattering the Soviet infantry units to his front. The Luftwaffe even provided some close air support sorties. However, the advance quickly stalled as Soviet resistance increased and Hoth was stopped well short of the Stalingrad perimeter. (Nik Cornish at www.Stavka.org.uk)

(6.Panzer-Division and 23.Panzer-Division), and the Romanian VI and VII corps. The 17.Panzer-Division was supposed to join the operation, but von Weichs proved reluctant to transfer it and tried to keep the division as an operational reserve around Millerovo.

Although the lead Panzergrenadier battalion of Raus' 6.Panzer-Division reached Kotelnikovo on 27 November, it took over a week for the rest of the division to arrive. Part of the division unloaded at Tatsinskaya and conducted a 230km road march, crossing the pontoon bridge over the Don at Tsimlianskaya, to reach Kotelnikovo. Obviously, this was not an efficient way to assemble a division for combat, but the single-track rail line to Kotelnikovo could not handle the amount of traffic demanded for a large-scale operation. Nor could the Luftwaffe provide much fighter support over Hoth's assembly areas, so it was fortunate that the VVS failed to conduct any battlefield interdiction strikes with its bombers to disrupt the vulnerable troop trains and road convoys. Eremenko was aware that German forces were assembling at Kotelnikovo and ordered Shapkin's 4th Cavalry Corps, reinforced with two tank brigades, to push south and either capture the railway station or at least disrupt German operations. By the time that Shapkin advanced south on 3 December, Raus had most of his division assembled and his tanks were in the process of unloading. Shapkin managed to push back some of Raus' outposts, but Raus counter-attacked on the morning of 4 December with his panzers and shattered the 81st Cavalry Division and 85th Tank Brigade. The Battle of Pokhlebin cost Shapkin over 2,000 troops and a number of tanks, which caused the rest of his corps to retreat towards the Aksai River. Raus lost at least five tanks and one Marder III destroyed. Kirchner wanted 6.Panzer-Division to pursue the retreating Soviets to the Aksai River, but Raus was reluctant to push north with only a few Romanian cavalrymen to guard his flanks. Although the lead elements of 23.Panzer-Division arrived south of Kotelnikovo on 28 November, the division required over a week to refit, receive replacement vehicles and move into position. Even then, 23.Panzer-Division could only field a brigade-size *Kampfgruppe*. It was not until 10 December that Kirchner had two combat-ready *Panzer-Divisionen* assembled, but adverse weather caused *Wintergewitter* to be postponed.

Hoth would have preferred to have delayed the attack further, until 17.Panzer-Division arrived, but von Manstein realized that the situation was slipping past the point of no return and ordered Hoth to commence the operation on 12 December with the forces to hand. Von Manstein was concerned not only about the Soviet attacks along the Chir River, but the evident failure of the Luftwaffe airlift to provide adequate supplies to 6.Armee. Although VIII.Fliegerkorps managed to deliver 362 tons of supplies on 7 December, on most days it delivered fewer than 100 tons. On some days, no flights arrived at all. Despite Göring's promises, the Luftwaffe was unable to meet 6.Armee's logistical requirements, which meant that the German forces in the pocket were rapidly losing their combat effectiveness. Von Manstein knew that in order for *Wintergewitter* to have a chance, 6.Armee still had to have the capability to conduct a breakout attack to meet the relief force.

At 0630hrs on 12 December, Hoth commenced *Wintergewitter*. The weather was cold, but skies were clear and visibility excellent. The 6.Panzer-Division, with 141 tanks, was the *Schwerpunkt*, pushing up the rail line, striking the centre of Trufanov's 51st Army. Raus was able to overrun the 302nd Rifle Division deployed on the rail line, then pivoted west to strike the remnants of Shapkin's 4th Cavalry Corps. Kamfgruppe Illig from 23.Panzer-Division, with 30 tanks, protected Raus' right flank and pushed back part of the 126th Rifle Division. Thanks to clear skies, the Luftwaffe was able to provide Hoth with close air support sorties, as well as bombing Soviet aircraft on the ground at Abganerovo. The VVS, fully committed to reducing the Stalingrad pocket, provided no sorties to support Trufanov's 51st Army. Under these favourable conditions, Hoth was able to advance about 20km on the first day of *Wintergewitter* and inflict serious losses on Trufanov's 51st Army. Eremenko reacted to *Wintergewitter* by moving Volskiy's 4th Mechanized Corps (81 tanks) to establish a blocking position at Verkhne Kumski and Tanaschishin's 13th Tank Corps (49 tanks) to Zutov.

Shortly after dawn on 13 December, Raus sent Kampfgruppe Hünersdorff to seize an unguarded ford across the Aksai River. Boldly pushing north to Verkhne Kumski, Hünersdorff bumped straight into the lead elements of the 4th Mechanized Corps around noon. The initial meeting engagement expanded into a protracted tank battle around Verkhne Kumski that would last five days, as the Soviets fed more forces into the area to stop the German advance. The 23.Panzer-Division became involved in a separate battle with the 13th Tank Corps, further to the east. Concerned by the German advance across the Aksai River, Stalin made several decisions that had a profound effect on the campaign. First, he ordered General-leytenant Rodion I. Malinovsky's 2nd Guards Army, which had been held back for use in the upcoming Operation *Saturn*, transferred to backstop Trufanov's 51st Army. As a result, Operation *Saturn* was reduced in scale to Operation *Little Saturn*. Second, Stalin ordered Rotmistrov's 7th Tank Corps transferred from Popov's

Soldiers from 6.Panzer-Division examine a knocked-out T-34 tank in the village of Verkhne-Kumskiy. Although Hoth finally achieved a tactical victory over the 4th Mechanized Corps, the Soviet delaying action enabled the 2nd Guards Army to reach the Myshkova River, blocking Hoth from reaching 6.Armee. (Author's collection)

5th Shock Army to reinforce Trufanov, which deprived Popov of his best strike unit just as he was winning on the Chir. Finally, Stalin ordered Eremenko to postpone the reduction of 6.Armee and focus on defeating Hoth's forces. Anxiety that somehow the Germans might deprive him of his triumph at Stalingrad caused Stalin to interfere with operations that were all on the verge of achieving decisive success. On the other side, Heeresgruppe B finally released 17.Panzer-Division, but it would take four days before it could join Hoth's forces.

Volskiy's 4th Mechanized Corps launched a major attack against Raus' 6.Panzer-Division at Verkhne Kumski on 15 December, forcing the Germans to fall back to their bridgehead over the Aksai. However, Raus counter-

A group of Romanian infantrymen supporting Hoth's armour during Operation *Wintergewitter*, mid-December 1942. The lack of reliable infantry units to guard the flanks of the advance is one of the factors that doomed the Stalingrad relief effort. (Author's collection)

attacked on 16 December, assisted by a large number of Luftwaffe air strikes. Nevertheless, 6.Panzer-Division failed to capture Verkhne Kumski and it was clear that Kirchner's LVII.Panzer-Korps was being drawn into a tactical quagmire. Volskiy's corps suffered heavy losses, but its troops put in a superb defensive performance that disrupted the tempo of the enemy offensive. The Germans also lost a significant amount of men and armoured vehicles around Verkhne Kumski, but it was the loss of time that fatally undermined any chance of *Wintergewitter* achieving success. The arrival of 17.Panzer-Division (with just 36 tanks) finally allowed Hoth to attack with three *Panzer-Divisionen* on 18 December, supported by Stuka strikes, but Volskiy's depleted 4th Mechanized Corps still managed to hold Verkhne Kumski for another day. Unknown to Hoth, Malinovsky's 2nd Guards Army was already forming a solid second line of defence along the Myshkova River with five fresh rifle divisions, and Rotmistrov's 7th Tank Corps was nearby. Hoth attacked again on 19 December, finally overwhelming Volskiy's corps, which fell back to the Myshkova River after losing over 5,500 casualties and about 70 tanks. The week-long Battle of Verkhne Kumski cost LVII.Panzer-Korps about 1,600 casualties and 33 tanks, which left Hoth with just 92 operational tanks. After seeing off Volskiy's corps, 17.Panzer-Division pushed forward Kampfgruppe Seitz to seize Nizhne Kumskii on the southern bank of the Myshkova. Raus sent Kampfgruppe Hünersdorff on a wide detour that succeeded in capturing an intact bridge over the Myshkova at Vasil'yevka at 2200hrs on 19 December. Shortly after crossing the Myshkova, 6.Panzer-Division encountered the 3rd Guards Rifle Division from 2nd Guards Army, which blocked any further advance.

At this point, von Manstein realized that Hoth was unlikely to reach Stalingrad with his depleted forces and his long vulnerable flanks protected by weak Romanian screening forces. Kampfgruppe Hünersdorff's bridgehead over the Myshkova was about 50km from the southern edge of the Stalingrad pocket, but it was clear that *Wintergewitter* had run out of steam.

Von Manstein had already sent his intelligence officer into the pocket to confer with Paulus about a breakout plan, dubbed *Donnerschlag* (*Thunderclap*), whereby 6.Armee would attack southwards to link up with Hoth's forces. On the evening of 19 December, von Manstein sent a radio signal to Paulus, directing 6.Armee to begin a breakout attack as soon as possible. Hube began to amass the armour of XIV.Panzer-Korps near the south-west corner of the pocket and intended to employ 14.Panzer-Division and 3.Infanterie-Divisionen (mot.) and 29.Infanterie-Divisionen (mot.) to lead the breakout. Although fuel was in short supply, Hube had at least 60 operational panzers and had a reasonable chance of breaking through the 57th Army forces near Karpovka and pushing perhaps 20km south. However Paulus demurred, making no decision at all, primarily because Hitler had not authorized a breakout operation. Nor did Paulus believe that 6.Armee had sufficient remaining combat power to conduct a successful breakout; he expected it to be a disaster. Paulus thought some troops might escape, but all of 6.Armee's equipment and most of its personnel would be lost and he would be blamed for an unauthorized withdrawal that resulted in catastrophe.

Von Manstein continued to press Paulus for the next four days to mount a breakout, but nothing happened. All the while, the Soviet 51st Army and 2nd Guards Army mounted attacks against Hoth's small bridgehead over the Myshkova, inflicting losses and threatening to smash in the thinly held flanks, but Hitler would not allow Hoth to withdraw from this exposed position. Raus' 6.Panzer-Division was soon reduced to just 41 operational tanks and was now badly outnumbered at Vasil'yevka; there was no hope of any further advance. By 23 December, it was clear that 6.Armee was beyond saving, and after one last fruitless appeal to Paulus, von Manstein quietly called off *Wintergewitter*. On the night of 23/24 December, Raus' 6.Panzer-Division began moving west across the Don bridge, in order to support Armee-Abteilung Hollidt. Hoth was left with a token force of two understrength *Panzer-Divisionen*, with a combined strength of just 28 operational tanks.

On the morning of 24 December, Eremenko's Stalingrad Front launched its Kotelnikovo offensive, with two rifle corps from Malinovsky's 2nd Guards Army attacking across the Myshkova River. Outnumbered by more than 8:1 in tanks and manpower, LVII.Panzer-Korps was forced to abandon its bridgehead at Vasil'yevka. Once across the Myshkova, Malinovsky began committing his armour, including Rotmistrov's 7th Tank Corps and the 2nd Guards Mechanized Corps, which together possessed over 300 tanks. The 51st Army attacked Hoth's right flank with infantry and the 3rd Guards Mechanized Corps. Under heavy pressure, Hoth conducted a fighting withdrawal to the Aksai River, suffering heavy losses along the way. On 25 December, the Soviets continued their offensive, striking both the Romanian VI Corps on Hoth's left flank and the Romanian VII Corps on his right flank. With the enemy flanks crumbling, Eremenko committed General-mayor Semen I. Bogdanov's fresh 6th Mechanized Corps (200 tanks) to strike the centre of the LVII.Panzer-Korps. After heavy fighting, the LVII.Panzer-Korps abandoned its positions on the Aksai River on the night of 26/27 December and fell back south along the rail line. Despite the arrival of SS-Panzergrenadier-Division Wiking, Hoth's forces were too depleted to hold Kotelnikovo, which was captured by Soviet tanks on the evening of 29 December. Although Hoth's forces escaped encirclement, both his *Panzer-Divisionen* had been decimated and were really no longer combat effective. Altogether, Hoth's forces suffered about 15,000 casualties in *Wintergewitter* and lost over 200 tanks. Furthermore, the inability of Hoth's weakened forces to stop the Stalingrad Front's push down the rail line meant that Heeresgruppe A in the Caucasus was now at serious risk of being outflanked and isolated. Reluctantly, Hitler acknowledged that the failure of *Wintergewitter* meant not only the loss of 6.Armee, but that Heeresgruppe A would have to withdraw from the Caucasus at once.

LITTLE SATURN, 16–28 DECEMBER 1942

Since early November, Vasilevskiy and his staff had been planning Operation *Saturn* as a follow-on offensive, which would commence after Operation *Uranus* encircled 6.Armee. The Stavka planning team designed *Saturn* as a two-phase operation. In the first phase, two Guards armies from Vatutin's South-Western Front were tasked with demolishing the Italian Eighth Army along the Don, while the 5th Tank Army completed the destruction of the 3rd Romanian Army and Armee-Abteilung Hollidt. In phase two, Vatutin would commit the fresh 2nd Guards Army to exploit the rupture in the Axis front by advancing up to 250km and thereby set the stage for the liberation of Rostov. Vatutin was provided with plentiful resources to conduct *Saturn*, which was intended to demolish the Axis position in southern Russia. On 8 December, Lelyushenko's 1st Guards Army was redesignated as the 3rd Guards Army and General-leytenant Vasily I. Kuznetsov took command of the new 1st Guards Army. Kuznetsov's 1st Guards Army was formed as a powerful strike force, comprising four tank corps (17th, 18th, 24th and 25th) and nine rifle divisions. Lelyushenko's 3rd Guards Army comprised the 1st Guards Mechanized Corps and seven rifle divisions. Romanenko's 5th Tank Army would also participate in a supporting role for *Saturn*, along with the 6th Army from the Voronezh Front. Altogether, Vatutin would command over 370,000 troops and 1,170 tanks, providing him with a large numerical superiority over the opposing Axis forces.

However, enemy actions began to affect the forces available for *Saturn*. Romanenko's 5th Tank Army suffered heavier-than expected casualties in the

Italian infantry with a captured Soviet 45mm M1937 anti-tank gun. Note that the crew are poorly dressed for a Russian winter, lacking greatcoats, gloves or winter camouflage. Furthermore, the anti-tank gun is deployed in the open, without any cover or concealment. (Nik Cornish at www.Stavka.org.uk)

Operation *Little Saturn*, 16–28 December 1942

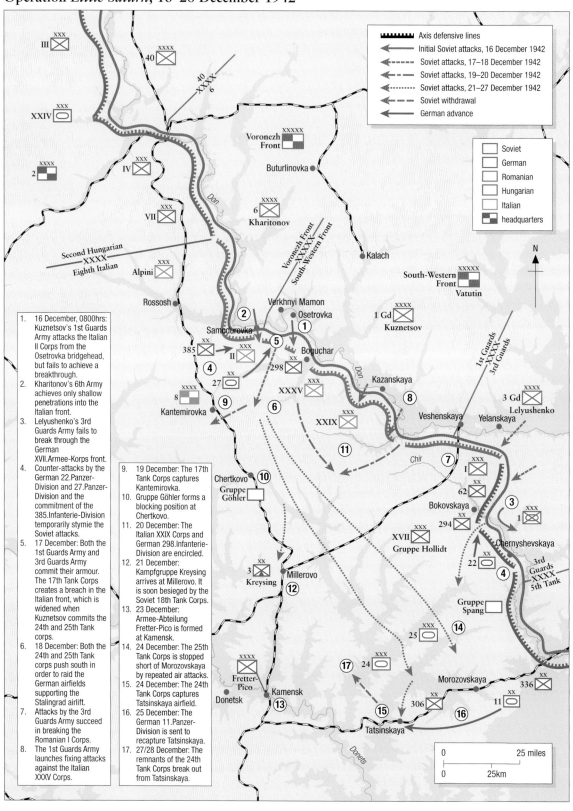

Legend:
- Axis defensive lines
- Initial Soviet attacks, 16 December 1942
- Soviet attacks, 17–18 December 1942
- Soviet attacks, 19–20 December 1942
- Soviet attacks, 21–27 December 1942
- Soviet withdrawal
- German advance

- Soviet
- German
- Romanian
- Hungarian
- Italian
- headquarters

N

1. 16 December, 0800hrs: Kuznetsov's 1st Guards Army attacks the Italian II Corps from the Osetrovka bridgehead, but fails to achieve a breakthrough.
2. Kharitonov's 6th Army achieves only shallow penetrations into the Italian front.
3. Lelyushenko's 3rd Guards Army fails to break through the German XVII.Armee-Korps front.
4. Counter-attacks by the German 22.Panzer-Division and 27.Panzer-Division and the commitment of the 385.Infanterie-Division temporarily stymie the Soviet attacks.
5. 17 December: Both the 1st Guards Army and 3rd Guards Army commit their armour. The 17th Tank Corps creates a breach in the Italian front, which is widened when Kuznetsov commits the 24th and 25th Tank corps.
6. 18 December: Both the 24th and 25th Tank corps push south in order to raid the German airfields supporting the Stalingrad airlift.
7. Attacks by the 3rd Guards Army succeed in breaking the Romanian I Corps.
8. The 1st Guards Army launches fixing attacks against the Italian XXXV Corps.

9. 19 December: The 17th Tank Corps captures Kantemirovka.
10. Gruppe Göhler forms a blocking position at Chertkovo.
11. 20 December: The Italian XXIX Corps and German 298.Infanterie-Division are encircled.
12. 21 December: Kampfgruppe Kreysing arrives at Millerovo. It is soon besieged by the Soviet 18th Tank Corps.
13. 23 December: Armee-Abteilung Fretter-Pico is formed at Kamensk.
14. 24 December: The 25th Tank Corps is stopped short of Morozovskaya by repeated air attacks.
15. 24 December: The 24th Tank Corps captures Tatsinskaya airfield.
16. 25 December: The German 11.Panzer-Division is sent to recapture Tatsinskaya.
17. 27/28 December: The remnants of the 24th Tank Corps break out from Tatsinskaya.

protracted fighting on the Chir, and its level of commitment to *Saturn* would be less than envisioned by Vasilevskiy. Furthermore, Stalin's decision to transfer Malinovsky's 2nd Guards Army to block Hoth's advance essentially deprived Saturn of the resources to reach Rostov, since it no longer had a large exploitation force. Consequently, Vasilevskiy was forced to reduce the scope of the operation, hence altering its designation to *Little Saturn*. Now, instead of Rostov, the final objective for *Little Saturn* was the German airfields at Morozovskaya and Tatsinskaya, as well as the supply base at Tormosin. Vasilevskiy expected the South-Western Front to achieve all its objectives within six days.

The primary target of *Little Saturn* was General Italo Gariboldi's Eighth Italian Army, which was defending a 125km-wide sector along the Don. Gariboldi's army consisted of ten Italian infantry divisions in three corps (II, XXXV and Alpini) and the German 298.Infanterie-Division. Since the Italians only had one battalion of light tanks, Heeresgruppe B cobbled together an ad hoc armoured unit designated as the 27.Panzer-Division, to serve as a mobile reserve for the Italians. In reality, 27.Panzer-Division was little more than a regimental-size battlegroup, equipped with 65 mostly obsolete tanks. Soviet pre-battle reconnaissance efforts alerted the Germans that an enemy offensive was imminent in this sector, so they began moving the 385.Infanterie-Division and 387.Infanterie-Division to further reinforce the Italians. A number of ad hoc battlegroups were also created to defend key points behind the lines – a lesson already learned from *Uranus*.

Vatutin began the operation at 0800hrs on 16 December, with a 90-minute artillery preparation, which was ineffective due to heavy fog. The adverse weather also forced the VVS to cancel its planned air strikes. As a result, the Soviet infantry began their assaults around 0930hrs against enemy defences that were not suppressed. General-mayor Fedor M. Kharitonov's 6th Army, attacking from the Samodurovka bridgehead with four rifle divisions, achieved only a 2km-deep penetration into the Italian Cosseria Division's front. Vatutin's main effort, delivered by Kuznetsov's 1st Guards Army from the Osetrovka bridgehead, massed three rifle divisions against the Italian Ravenna Division and one regiment of the German 298.Infanterie-Division. Despite a massive imbalance in numbers and fire support, Kuznetsov's infantry experienced great difficulty penetrating the enemy's defences. When Kuznetsov tried to move tanks from the 18th Tank Corps forward to support the infantry, they ran into uncleared minefields and lost 27 tanks. The 27.Panzer-Division even managed an afternoon counter-attack, which further disrupted the Soviet offensive tempo and limited Kuznetsov's army to only minor gains on the first day of *Little Saturn*. Likewise, Lelyushenko's 3rd Guards Army attacked with the 14th Guards Rifle Corps, but failed to dent the German XVII.Armee-Korps defence on the upper Chir. The 22.Panzer-Division, with about a dozen tanks, launched a counter-attack that pushed back Lelyushenko's infantry. It was not an auspicious start to *Little Saturn*.

Chagrined by the initial lack of progress, Vatutin ordered 1st Guards Army and 3rd Guards Army to begin committing their armour on the second day of *Little Saturn*, in order to create a breakthrough. On 17 December, Kuznetsov fed the 17th Tank Corps into the battle at the boundary between the Cosseria and Ravenna divisions. The fighting raged all day, but despite the efforts of 27.Panzer-Division and a regiment of German infantry, the

An Italian Fiat L6/40 light tank that came to grief along an icy road during the retreat from the Don in mid-December 1942. The Italian XXXV Corps had one battalion of these light tanks, but they were no match for Soviet tanks. (From the fonds of the RGAKFD in Krasnogorsk via Stavka)

Soviets finally breached the main Axis defensive line late on the second day of the offensive. Kuznetsov immediately moved General-major Petr R. Pavlov's 25th Tank Corps into the breach, followed soon thereafter by General-major Vasily M. Badanov's 24th Tank Corps. Lelyushenko's 3rd Guards Army committed its 1st Guards Mechanized Corps, but still failed to breach the line held by the German XVII.Armee-Korps. Once the Italian front was broken, Vatutin ordered the boldest phase of *Little Saturn* – deep armoured raids to capture the airfields involved in the Stalingrad airlift. While the rest of 6th Army and 1st Guards Army focused on widening the breach in Italian lines, Pavlov's 25th Tank Corps pushed south toward Morozovskaya airfield, while Badanov's 24th Tank Corps headed for Tatsinskaya airfield; both of these objectives lay about 240km from the operational start line. Vatutin had hoped that these two tank corps could advance over 50km per day, but this proved impossible in deep snow and with limited fuel supplies. Although the two Soviet tank corps had been provided with two loads of fuel and ammunition, they could expect no further logistic support until after they reached their objectives.

Kuznetsov's 1st Guards Army kept up the pressure on 18 December and gradually widened the breach in the Italian front, despite desperate resistance by 298.Infanterie-Division and 27.Panzer-Division. Lelyushenko's 3rd Guards Army finally achieved success against the Romanian I Corps, which protected Armee-Abteilung Hollidt's left flank. After strong attacks by infantry and tanks from the 1st Guards Mechanized Corps, both the Romanian 7th and 11th Infantry divisions collapsed. The Soviet 1st Guards Mechanized Corps boldly advanced and linked up with 18th Tank Corps from 1st Guards Army at Koshary, which isolated the Italian XXXV Army Corps. The German 62.Infanterie-Division and part of the 298.Infanterie-Division were also surrounded. By the end of 19 December, the Italian Eighth Army was disintegrating, with most of its units falling back in disorder. Only the Italian Alpini Corps remained solid. During the day, General-mayor Pavel P. Poluboyarov's 17th Tank Corps fought its way into Kantemirovka, a major Italian logistics base. Kuznetsov's army pursued the retreating Italian units, taking several thousand prisoners.

Heeresgruppe B tried to form resistance centres in key positions in order to delay Vatutin's advance, while transferring reinforcements from other sectors. Gruppe Göhler (which included part of 385.Infanterie-Division and some SS-Police units) blocked the area south of Kantemirovka and formed a hedgehog at Chertkovo. Although the Chertkovo garrison was surrounded by 22 December, it effectively tied up one of Kuznetsov's rifle corps and prevented Soviet exploitation to the south-west. The Italian Alpini Corps and small units like the Führer-Begleit-Bataillon (FBB) managed to block the Soviet 6th Army from rolling up the open right Axis flank north of Kantemirovka. Although small, the FBB was heavily armed with 7.5cm anti-tank guns and a company of Panzer IV tanks. Von Weichs also arranged for 19.Panzer-Division to move to reinforce the Kantemirovka sector, although it would take nearly a week to arrive. Meanwhile German reinforcements trickled into the sector, and von Weichs dispatched them to threatened areas. Kampfgruppe Kreysing from Generalmajor Hans Kreysing's 3.Gebirgs-Division was en route to Hoth's forces, but was re-routed to defend the vital airbase and supply depot at Millerovo on 21 December. Kreysing arrived and established a hedgehog defence of the airbase with Gebirgsjäger-Regiment 144, two artillery battalions, and some Pionier and Flak troops. Part of the VII./Leibstandarte SS Adolf Hitler Wachbataillon arrived from Berlin and was incorporated into Kampfgruppe Kreysing just before Bakharov's 18th Tank Corps encircled Millerovo. Soviet probing attacks on 24–25 December confirmed that Millerovo was heavily defended, and Bakharov's corps shifted to a siege operation until infantry arrived – which further disrupted Kuznetsov's operational tempo. Kreysing's stand in Millerovo bought time for Generalleutnant Maximilian Fretter-Pico to form Armee-Abteilung Fretter-Pico in Kamensk on the Donets. Fretter-Pico only had a few battalions from 304.Infanterie-Division arriving from Belgium, but this was just enough to begin building a new front behind the Donets.

While Kuznetsov's advance was slowing down due to the friction caused by unexpected Axis resistance, Badanov's 24th Tank Corps and Pavlov's 25th Tank Corps were closing in on their objectives, although they were well behind schedule. Unknown to them, the German 306.Infanterie-Division had just arrived at Tatsinskaya and elements were deployed north of the airfields to delay the approaching Soviet armour. Pavlov's spearhead bumped into Gruppe Spang, which included an infantry battalion from 306. Infanterie-Division, 30km north of Morozovskaya. The German blocking unit had some 7.5cm anti-tank guns, which they used to knock out nine Soviet tanks. Pavlov deployed his corps on line and overran a German battalion, but Gruppe Spang called for Stuka support and the Luftwaffe inflicted significant damage on the exposed Soviet columns. Pavlov managed to shove his forces past Gruppe Spang, but further Stuka attacks halted his corps short of its objective. Farther west, Badanov's 24th Tank Corps fought its way past Kampfgruppe von Heinemann (Luftwaffe Flak troops) and attacked Tatsinskaya airfield on the morning of 24 December. The VIII. Fliegerkorps personnel were caught completely by surprise and the impact of the first Soviet shells incited a panic. The flight line at Tatsinskaya was packed with nearly 200 transport aircraft when a battalion of Soviet tanks arrived, firing as they moved. The Luftwaffe transports began emergency sorties, which managed to save a large number of aircraft, but over 50 planes were destroyed and large stockpiles of supplies were lost. Badanov informed Vatutin that he had captured Tatsinskaya, but his remaining 58 tanks were low on fuel and ammunition. However, Vatutin was in no position to provide immediate assistance since the nearest Soviet forces, Lelyushenko's 3rd Guards Army, were still about 65km distant. Essentially, both of the Soviet tank corps committed to deep-battle missions were left stranded and forced to await relief from the rest of the South-Western Front.

The loss of Tatsinskaya airfield provoked a crisis in Heeresgruppe Don because it seriously disrupted the airlift to Stalingrad and threatened to sever the army group's lines of communication. Von Manstein had already decided to transfer 6.Panzer-Division from Hoth's command to deal with *Little Saturn* and now Hollidt was forced to commit his only mobile reserve,

The Battle of the Stalingrad Pocket, 1–31 December 1942

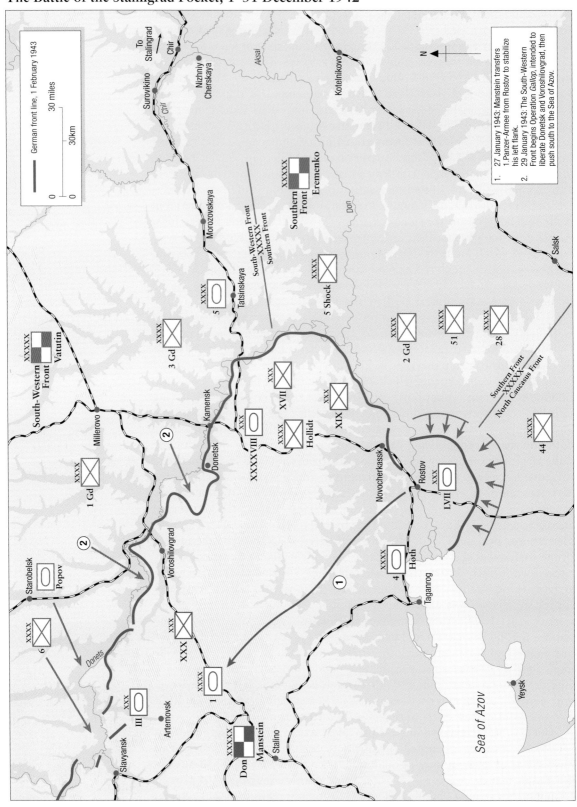

Balck's 11.Panzer-Division. Balck quickly surrounded Badanov's corps by 25 December, but let the Luftwaffe soften them up with repeated air strikes. Rather than mount a direct assault, the Germans gradually blasted Badanov's raiding force into pieces. Without authorization, Badanov conducted a breakout on the night of 27/28 December and succeeded in reaching Soviet lines with nine tanks and about 900 of his men. Both the 24th and 25th Tank corps were essentially destroyed in these raids, but they did seriously degrade the Luftwaffe's airlift operations to 6.Armee.

STALINGRAD *KESSELSCHLACHT*, 1–31 DECEMBER 1942

Although Paulus had managed to establish a fairly strong outer perimeter by the end of November, Stavka was initially confident that Rokossovsky's Don Front would be able to reduce the *Kessel* (pocket) with some help from Eremenko's Stalingrad Front. Consequently, Rokossovsky ordered Chistiakov's 21st Army and Batov's 65th Army to begin probing attacks against the west side of the pocket on 1 December. At this point, Heitz's VIII. Armee-Korps held the line with four infantry divisions (44., 76., 113. and 376.) while Hube's XIV.Panzer-Korps held the Marinovka salient with two motorized infantry divisions (3. and 29.) and 14.Panzer-Division. Hube kept a small tactical reserve, consisting of a *Panzer-Bataillon* and a *Kradschützen* (motorcycle) battalion, to deal with enemy breakthroughs. Initially, the Soviets probed the German front with battalion-size attacks, which then escalated to regimental-size attacks. The weather, a mix of freezing rain, fog and snowstorms, favoured infiltration attacks. On the morning of 2 December, the 21st Army attacked the Marinovka salient with shock groups from three rifle divisions (96th, 293rd and 51st Guards Rifle Division) and tanks from Kravchenko's 4th Tank Corps, which succeeded in creating two breaches in the line. A rapid German counter-attack succeeded in restoring the front, but at great cost, including at least one tank, two Marder IIs and one assault gun destroyed, as well as ten more tanks damaged. At the same time, Galanin's 24th Army and Batov's 65th Army attacked the 44.Infanterie-Division with shock groups from four rifle divisions, supported by tanks. The German infantry held their ground, but suffered significant casualties.

By 3 December, Soviet attacks were intensifying around the perimeter, as Eremenko's Stalingrad Front launched attacks with Chuikov's 62nd Army, Shumilov's 64th Army and Tolbukhin's 57th Army. Despite the woeful conditions of Chuikov's units, the 62nd Army managed to inflict 679 casualties on Seydlitz's LI.Armee-Korps in three days of fighting in Stalingrad. Rokossovsky launched a much larger offensive on 4 December, with four rifle divisions from Batov's 65th Army attacking 44.Infanterie-Division, while two rifle divisions from Chistiakov's 21st Army attacked 376.Infanterie-Division. Batov's shock groups crushed one of 44.Infanterie-Division's battalions and nearly achieved a breakthrough, but Hube committed his armour reserve and two battalions

German troops move cautiously past the wreck of a knocked out T-34 tank, which appears to have been destroyed by a hollow charge. Although many German troops inside the perimeter became passive due to cold and hunger, there were a number of aggressive fighters who remained well armed and relatively well fed right to the end. (Nik Cornish at www. Stavka.org.uk)

A group of Panzer III tanks from 3.Infanterie-Division (mot.) in a reserve position near the Marinovka in early December 1942. The 6.Armee used its remaining panzers as a mobile strike force to counter any enemy attempts to penetrate the west side of the pocket. As long as the fuel and ammunition lasted, this tactic only helped to delay the inevitable. (Bundesarchiv, Bild 101I-451-0899-35; Foto: Niermann/Herber)

of assault guns in well-timed counter-attacks, which halted the Soviet advance. Losses were heavy on both sides. Hube's XIV.Panzer-Korps claimed to have destroyed 59 enemy tanks and Soviet personnel casualties were probably over 2,000. The German units on the western front suffered 1,035 casualties in two days of fighting and lost a significant number of armoured fighting vehicles. While the results of the fighting on 4–5 December were frustrating for Rokossovsky, the cost to the defenders in terms of fuel and ammunition expended was prohibitive – 6.Armee simply could not fight this type of battle for very long.

After a two-day pause, the Don and Stalingrad fronts renewed their attacks on 8 December. Chistiakov's 21st Army attacked the Marinovka salient and the boundary between VIII.Armee-Korps and XIV.Panzer-Korps, while Batov's 65th Army attacked 44.Infanterie-Division again. The Soviets used their armour in small groups, in the infantry support role. Once again, counter-attacks by Hube's panzer reserves arrived in time to prevent a breakthrough, and claimed to have knocked out another 72 enemy tanks. However, German losses in two days of fighting on the western front were 718, including 266 killed or missing. The front-line German infantry divisions, with their troops freezing on the open steppe, could not sustain these kinds of losses for long. Paulus and his corps commanders kept drafting personnel from support units to replace infantry losses, which meant that the combat effectiveness of 6.Armee's infantry units relied increasingly on a handful of remaining veteran junior leaders. On the other side of the hill, Stavka had expected to commence an all-out offensive to reduce the Stalingrad pocket by mid-December, but the start of *Wintergewitter* forced the Soviets to postpone this effort in favour of stopping Hoth's relief operation. Consequently, a temporary lull settled over the pocket during 11–15 December.

As fighting flared around the perimeter of the *Kessel*, the fate of 6.Armee increasingly hung on the slender thread provided by the Luftwaffe's airlift operations. In the first week of the airlift, VIII.Fliegerkorps was only able to deliver 515 tons of supplies. Once more aircraft arrived at Tatsinskaya and Morozovskaya, VIII.Fliegerkorps was able to increase its daily supply deliveries, but it never came close to meeting 6.Armee's logistical requirements. On 7 December, VIII.Fliegerkorps managed to deliver 362 tons of supplies, but Soviet fighters shot down 15 transports. The next day, the Luftwaffe delivered 209 tons, but lost another 20 transports to enemy action.

General-major Timofei T. Khriukhin's 8th Air Army was able to establish an effective air blockade around Stalingrad, which made it increasingly prohibitive for the Luftwaffe to attempt daylight resupply flights into the pocket. Soviet bombers and Il-2 Sturmoviks also harassed the airbases involved in the airlift incessantly, inflicting damage and losses that prevented the Luftwaffe from achieving its quota. Although VIII.Fliegerkorps tried to use its limited number of fighters to escort transports, this did not prove practical. Consequently, the transport groups shifted to flying into the pocket at night and during snowstorms, which led to more accidents and less tonnage delivered. Nor did the Luftwaffe do a very good job evacuating wounded personnel from the pocket; many return flights arrived back at Tatsinskaya half-empty. In one last surge, VIII.Fliegerkorps managed to deliver 850 tons of supplies on 19–21 December, but thereafter the airlift began to fall apart due to the friction imposed by enemy action and adverse weather.

Dead Germans lie next to their 2cm Flak gun in the snow. Pickert's 9.Flak-Division fought as ground troops in the Stalingrad pocket and their guns were used to break up many attacks. However, the guns were mostly stationary by mid-December due to a lack of fuel and transport. (Courtesy of the Central Museum of the Armed Forces, Moscow via Stavka)

Contrary to some popular accounts, some units in 6.Armee had received winter clothing prior to encirclement and cold-weather injuries were not a major problem for most of December. Until 25 December, daytime ranges hovered around 32° F (0° C), but could drop to 14° F (-10° C) at night. Frostbite accounted for only about 4–8 per cent of 6.Armee's total casualties, although many other soldiers were ill. On 25 December, temperatures dropped to well below freezing, both during the day and at night. The 6.Armee still had plenty of horses to eat in December and the Luftwaffe flew in just enough food to prevent starvation, but the malnourished troops were surviving on quarter-rations. Due to heavy losses, the Germans were forced to disband some units and combine the survivors with other units, which is what happened with

Soviet troops moving through the jagged wreckage of the Krasny Oktyabr Steel Plant. Note the concertina wire in the front. Although Chuikov ordered his 62nd Army to keep attacking throughout the final weeks of the campaign, they gained little ground until 6.Armee began to fall apart under the hammer blows of Operation *Ring*. (Author's collection)

A knocked-out KV-1 heavy tank in central Stalingrad, covered with new fallen snow. There were few resources in this devastated wasteland for the encircled 6.Armee to draw upon. (Author's collection)

94.Infanterie-Division on the north-east side of the pocket. There were also 13,000 Romanian troops in the pocket, who were integrated into German combat units. Although a number of the Hiwis abandoned the encircled 6.Armee, over 19,000 remained loyal and some even participated in combat, fighting against the Red Army. Amazingly, 6.Armee still had 103 operational tanks and 35 assault guns in mid-December and there was still enough fuel for defensive operations, but ammunition stocks were dwindling.

As Hoth's panzers pushed north towards Stalingrad, Rokossovsky and Eremenko were ordered to resume attacks on 6.Armee in order to prevent a breakout attempt. Strong attacks on the western front and the Marinovka salient on 19 December inflicted 1,141 casualties on 6.Armee, but German defences held. Eremenko also ensured that Tolbukhin's 57th Army – which lay in the sector from which 6.Armee would most likely attempt a breakout – was reinforced with additional rifle units and tanks. On 25 December, Zhadov's 66th Army mounted a surprise attack against the north-east corner of the pocket, near Orlovka. Under cover of a snowstorm, two Soviet regiments and 14 tanks attacked at dawn and captured a key hilltop from 16.Panzer-Division. A German armoured counter-attack not only failed to recapture the position, but suffered heavy losses from enemy artillery and anti-tank fire. Three days later, Rokossovsky attacked the western front again with five rifle divisions, and nearly broke through 376.Infanterie-Division. Hube's panzers conducted a night counter-attack on 29 December, led by Oberstleutnant Willy Langkeit, which was partially successful. However, Langkeit had five tanks destroyed and ten more damaged, which seriously reduced Hube's panzer reserve. Furthermore, fuel and ammunition reserves were now dangerously low.

During the course of December 1942, 6.Armee suffered almost 22,000 casualties, including 6,914 dead or missing. Since the army received few replacements after encirclement, it strength was in sharp decline. Although the encircled 6.Armee had fended off multiple attacks and lost very little ground, it was now a wounded animal, waiting for a killing blow. With the bread ration reduced to just 80g on 30 December, starvation was just around the corner. By 25 December everyone in the army knew that rescue was no longer on the cards. Incredibly, morale was still intact in 6.Armee and some personnel who had been caught outside the pocket continued to volunteer to fly in to join their units. A large part of the remarkable psychological glue that held the Wehrmacht together in adversity, *Kameradschaften* (comradeship), was on full display during the final weeks of 6.Armee, which was inexorably heading towards annihilation.

OPERATION *RING* AND THE END OF 6.ARMEE, 1 JANUARY–2 FEBRUARY 1943

Although *Wintergewitter* temporarily distracted Stavka from the task of completing the destruction of 6.Armee, it was not forgotten. While

A German 15cm sFH18 howitzer lies forlorn in the snow. The German division- and corps-level artillery was still effective in the first few days of Operation *Ring* but soon fell silent due to lack of ammunition. Note the howitzer in the background being pulled by horses. Without artillery support, 6.Armee's defence rapidly collapsed. (Author's collection)

Vasilevskiy focused on coordinating *Little Saturn* and the pursuit of Hoth's forces, Stavka assigned General-polkovnik Nikolai N. Voronov to coordinate the final battle at Stalingrad. Voronov was chief of the Red Army's artillery, and he vowed to use massed firepower to smash 6.Armee's defences, rather than rely just on the standard tank–infantry attacks that had heretofore achieved so little. He submitted a plan for the final offensive, Operation *Ring* (*Kol'tso*), to Stavka on 27 December, which was actually just a scaled-up version of the attacks that Rokossovsky and Eremenko had conducted in early December. Zhukov took a hand in revising the plan, as well as Rokossovsky and Eremenko. The revised plan, completed on 29–30 December, simplified command and control by transferring the 57th, 62nd and 64th armies to the Don Front; hence, Rokossovsky would solely command the final operation. The remainder of Eremenko's Stalingrad Front was redesignated as the Southern Front and tasked with pursuing Hoth. Operation *Ring* would commence with a massive attack by the 21st, 24th and 65th armies to break 6.Armee's western front, then pivot to cut off the Marinovka salient. Altogether, these three armies would commit 19 rifle divisions, while the other four armies (57th, 62nd, 64th and 65th) would conduct supporting attacks with another 21 rifle divisions. Rokossovsky expected that simultaneous concentric attacks would break 6.Armee into several smaller chunks, which could be destroyed in one week of heavy fighting.

While preparing for Operation *Ring*, the Don Front kept up the pressure on 6.Armee, conducting small-scale attacks in early January. As a result, 6.Armee suffered another 4,265 casualties between 1 and 9 January. While Soviet losses were also heavy, Stavka provided Rokossovsky with 20,000 replacements to replenish his infantry units, which enabled him to increase his front-line rifle divisions to about 60 per cent of their authorized strength. Altogether, the Don Front comprised over 281,000

A burnt-out T-34 tank. Rokossovsky lost about half his armour in the first week of Operation *Ring*, due to the unexpected resistance of 6.Armee's remaining anti-tank guns. Indeed, throughout the final weeks of the campaign, Soviet leaders tended to underestimate the enemy's power of resistance. (Nik Cornish at www.Stavka.org.uk)

SOVIET

A. 7th Rifle Corps
B. 169th Rifle Division
C. 157th Rifle Division
D. 204th Rifle Division
E. 36th Guards Rifle Division
F. 38th Rifle Division
G. 422nd Rifle Division
H. 115th Fortified Region
I. 15th Guards Rifle Division
J. 120th Rifle Division
K. 52nd Guards Rifle Division
L. 96th Rifle Division
M. 298th Rifle Division
N. 277th Rifle Division
O. 293rd Rifle Division
P. 51st Guards Rifle Division
Q. 173rd Rifle Division
R. 304th Rifle Division
S. 24th Rifle Division
T. 27th Guards Rifle Division
U. 214th Rifle Division
V. 273rd Rifle Division
W. 49th Rifle Division
X. 233rd Rifle Division
Y. 260th Rifle Division
Z. 343rd Rifle Division

65TH ARMY
21ST ARMY
21ST ARMY
57TH ARMY

MORNING 10 JAN
EVENING 10/11 JAN
DMITRIYEVKA
EVENING 11/12 JAN

KARPOVKA RIVER
MARINOVKA
KARPOVKA

NO ROGA
CHERVL RIV

24 | XXXX | GALANIN
65 | XXXX | BATOV
21 | XXXX | CHISTIAKOV

▼ EVENTS

10 January 1943

1. 0900hrs: The 21st Army attacks the Marinovka salient with three rifle divisions and penetrates the 29.Infanterie-Division defence.

2. 0900hrs: The 65th Army attacks the 44.Infanterie-Division with five rifle divisions and 90 tanks, which smashes the defence and achieves several deep penetrations.

3. 0900hrs: The 24th Army attacks the left flank of the 76.Infanterie-Division with two rifle divisions and gains 2km.

4. The 64th Army attacks the sector held by the Romanian 20th Infantry Division and one regiment of the 297.Infanterie-Division across the Karavatka balka.

5. The 57th Army attacks to isolate the German garrison in Tsybenko.

6. The Germans evacuate the Marinovka nose on the night of 10/11 January.

11 January

7. German assault guns and artillery fire prevent a breakthrough in the VIII.Armee-Korps sector.

8. German tanks and 8.8cm guns knock out 18 Churchill tanks from the 47th Guards Tank Regiment east of Dmitreyevka.

9. The XIV.Panzer-Korps and VIII.Armee-Korps conduct a withdrawal under heavy pressure toward the Rossoshka River valley.

12 January

10. 65th Army commits its second-echelon units, which reach the Rossosh River.

11. The 57th Army continues to attack the German strongpoint at Tsybenko and the 422nd Rifle Division eventually captures the town.

13 January

12. Rokossovsky shifts his main effort south and uses three rifle divisions from the 21st Army to capture Karpovka.

13. The 57th Army's 15th Guards Rifle Division attacks and seizes Staryi Rogachik, jeopardizing the German position on the Chervlenaya River.

14. The 38th Rifle Division, supported by tanks, advances north towards Bassargino station, rupturing the IV.Armee-Korps front.

14 January

15. The 65th Army's initial assault on Baburkin is repulsed by VIII.Armee-Korps.

16. The 57th Army captures Karpovka station and Novyi Rogachev.

15 January

17. With his western front disintegrating, Paulus orders the remnants of the VIII. Armee-Korps and XIV.Panzer-Korps to abandon the Rossoshka line.

18. 57th Army captures Bassargino station.

19. The 65th Army captures Elkhi.

16 January

20. The 21st Army pursues the retreating German units and the 51st Guards Rifle Division captures Pitomnik airfield.

THE FIRST PHASE OF OPERATION *RING*, 10–16 JANUARY 1943

The Don Front launched its final offensive to crush the 6.Armee by attacking the west side of the Stalingrad pocket, but enemy resistance was fiercer than expected. Although the Soviet attacks forced 6.Armee to pull back towards the city, the Don Front had to pause its offensive after one week.

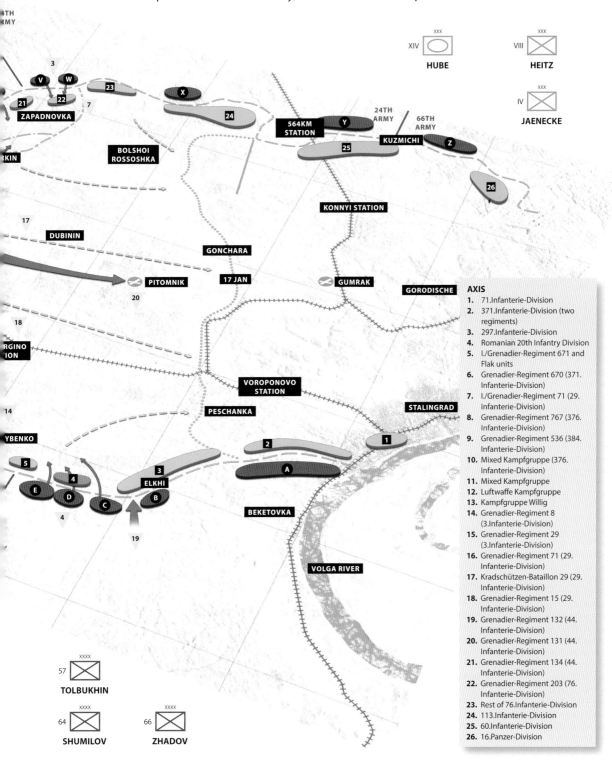

AXIS

1. 71.Infanterie-Division
2. 371.Infanterie-Division (two regiments)
3. 297.Infanterie-Division
4. Romanian 20th Infantry Division
5. I./Grenadier-Regiment 671 and Flak units
6. Grenadier-Regiment 670 (371. Infanterie-Division)
7. I./Grenadier-Regiment 71 (29. Infanterie-Division)
8. Grenadier-Regiment 767 (376. Infanterie-Division)
9. Grenadier-Regiment 536 (384. Infanterie-Division)
10. Mixed Kampfgruppe (376. Infanterie-Division)
11. Mixed Kampfgruppe
12. Luftwaffe Kampfgruppe
13. Kampfgruppe Willig
14. Grenadier-Regiment 8 (3.Infanterie-Division)
15. Grenadier-Regiment 29 (3.Infanterie-Division)
16. Grenadier-Regiment 71 (29. Infanterie-Division)
17. Kradschützen-Bataillon 29 (29. Infanterie-Division)
18. Grenadier-Regiment 15 (29. Infanterie-Division)
19. Grenadier-Regiment 132 (44. Infanterie-Division)
20. Grenadier-Regiment 131 (44. Infanterie-Division)
21. Grenadier-Regiment 134 (44. Infanterie-Division)
22. Grenadier-Regiment 203 (76. Infanterie-Division)
23. Rest of 76.Infanterie-Division
24. 113.Infanterie-Division
25. 60.Infanterie-Division
26. 16.Panzer-Division

Note: gridlines are shown at intervals of 10km (6.2 miles)

A pair of frozen German Landsers in the snow. Although daytime temperatures in the Stalingrad pocket averaged around 14° F (-10° C) in December 1942 and January 1943, there were nights when the temperatures dropped to as low as -31° F (-35° C), which was devastating for troops caught out in the open. Without adequate food or the ability to warm up, the fighting ability of German front-line troops along the western perimeter rapidly declined as the weather worsened. (Author's collection)

troops, which only slightly outnumbered the encircled 6.Armee. Rokossovsky was also provided with a great deal of artillery from the RVGK, enabling a greater concentration of firepower than heretofore employed in any single attack on the Eastern Front. Unlike previous offensives, the Don Front would not mass its available armour, but instead disperse it in the infantry support role in small groups. Altogether, the Don Front had 264 tanks for Operation *Ring*, which included five Guards tank regiments equipped with 110 KV-1 heavy tanks and the 47th Guards Tank Regiment equipped with 21 British-built Churchill tanks. The 16th Air Army would support the offensive with 400 aircraft. The Germans were aware of Soviet preparations for a major attack on the western sector, so Paulus transferred more of his remaining tanks and anti-tank guns to reinforce the threatened area. On 30 December, the 6.Armee quartermasters had issued most of their remaining fuel, providing one full load for the remaining operational tanks and assault guns. Artillery units had about 40 rounds left per howitzer, enough for one last fight. At this point, 6.Armee still held a perimeter that was 53km across its east–west axis and 35km north to south; this was far too much terrain to defend, but Hitler would not authorize Paulus to voluntarily shorten his lines. On 7 January, Rokossovsky sent a surrender ultimatum via envoys to Paulus, which was quickly rejected. The 6.Armee now knew that there would be no rescue, but rather a fight to the death.

Despite the recovery of Tatsinskaya airfield, VIII.Fliegerkorps shifted most of its airlift operations to Salsk airfield, which was further away. In an effort to boost the capacity of the air bridge, the Luftwaffe leadership began sending a wider variety of aircraft to be used as transports. On 9 January, seven Fw 200 Condor bombers flew into Pitomnik to deliver 36 tons of supplies; unlike the 2-ton capacity on the Ju 52, the Fw 200 was capable of carrying up to 5 tons. However, the Condors ran into trouble the next day, losing five aircraft to enemy fighters and accidents. The Luftwaffe also sent the prototype of the four-engine Ju 290 transport, which could carry up to 10 tons on one sortie. Although the aircraft had only made its first flight four months previously, the Ju 290 was pressed into combat service. It landed at Pitomnik on 10 January and carried out 78 wounded men on one flight. However, three days later, the Ju 290 crashed after take-off, killing five aircrew and 40 passengers.

Unlike operations *Uranus* and *Little Saturn*, Operation *Ring* began under favourable weather conditions that allowed Soviet forward observers to properly direct their artillery. The morning of 10 January was a cold but beautiful winter day, with light overcast and good visibility. Rokossovsky began a 55-minute artillery preparation against the western side of the pocket at 0805hrs, which inflicted great damage on the German positions, particularly in the 44.Infanterie-Division sector. Voronov had massed 500 guns/howitzers and 450 multiple rocket launchers across a 12km-wide attack sector – the highest Soviet artillery density yet achieved in the war. Sturmoviks from 16th Air Army also bombed and strafed German positions behind the main line of resistance. Then, at 0900hrs, Batov's 65th Army began its ground assault by hurling five rifle divisions and 90 heavy tanks against 44.Infanterie-Division. The German infantry fought desperately, sometimes hand-to-hand for some positions, but four battalions were smashed. Nor were the handful of operational German tanks and assault guns able to reverse enemy gains. Gradually, Batov's divisions succeeded in capturing a number of German positions

Soldiers from the 39th Guards Rifle Division move along the rail line near the Krasny Oktyabr Steel Plant, during Operation *Ring*. Chuikov's troops did not drive the German 79.Infanterie-Division out of the plant until 10 January 1943 – over 11 weeks since the enemy gained a foothold in the facility. (Author's collection)

and advancing up to 4km, but they did not quite break the VIII.Armee-Korps front. Chistiakov's 21st Army attacked the Marinovka salient with three rifle divisions and bit deeply into the flank of 29.Infanterie-Division (mot.). Galanin's 24th Army, attacked the German 76.Infanterie-Division with three rifle divisions and also gained some ground. By midday, it was clear that at least ten German infantry battalions had been badly mauled and that VIII.Armee-Korps was unlikely to maintain a continuous front for much longer. Each of the rest of Rokossovsky's armies launched their own attacks. In the south, the 57th and 64th armies managed to inflict significant damage on the German IV.Armee-Korps and penetrated up to 3km into the German defence.

Before dawn on 11 January, Hube quietly pulled his XIV.Panzer-Korps back 3km from the nose of the Marinovka salient, to avoid envelopment by Chistiakov's 21st Army. Once the sun rose, Rokossovsky kept up the pressure, pounding away at VIII.Armee-Korps, which managed to establish a thin defensive line in the Rossoshka River valley around Baburkin. Batov's 65th Army pushed into a gap north of the village of Dmitriyevka, which threatened to outflank Hube's XIV.Panzer-Korps. Only Kampfgruppe Reinbrecht (170 men, one 8.8cm Flak and two 7.5cm-equipped SdKfz 251/9 half-tracks) and Hauptmann Rudolf Haen's four tanks stood in the path of the Soviet advance. Emboldened, the Soviet tanks and infantry advanced over open ground and discovered that the German troops were still full of fight. Haen's veteran panzers shot the attacking Soviet 57th Guards Tank Regiment to pieces, knocking out 18 of its 21 British-built Churchill tanks. The German position held for the moment, although other units were falling back under pressure. Chistiakov's 21st Army forced 3.Infanterie-Division (mot.) to pull back, but suffered over 800 casualties in its attacking rifle divisions. Despite some tactical successes, Hube's XIV.Panzer-Korps had lost 30 of its 46 tanks and 11 of its 18 heavy anti-tank guns in the first two days of Operation *Ring*. Along the rest of the western front, the assault guns from Sturmgeschütz-Abteilung 177 and Sturmgeschütz-Abteilung 244 played a major role in preventing an immediate breakthrough by the 24th and 65th armies, but also lost a number of StuG IIIs. German artillery, though constrained by ammunition shortages, was still able to fire final protective fire missions which broke up Soviet infantry attacks.

How the Red Army found Pitomnik airfield on 16 January 1943 – scattered aircraft wreckage on a frozen steppe. Even before it was overrun, the airfield was under regular air and artillery bombardment, which turned the primitive airstrip into a shambles. (Author's collection)

Despite inflicting heavy losses on the attacking enemy, Hube's XIV. Panzer-Korps was forced to conduct a fighting withdrawal on 12 January, falling back 7km and pursued by Chistiakov's 21st Army. The 3.Infanterie-Division (mot) lost a good deal of its equipment in the withdrawal and was forced to blow up a number of tanks and vehicles for lack of fuel. A handful of still-operational Marder II tank destroyers kept enemy tanks at bay, destroying several of them. In the south, the Soviet 57th and 64th armies fought a protracted battle for the IV.Armee-Korps' strongpoint in Tsybenko, and gradually ground down the German defence in this sector. Although 6.Armee was clearly weakening, in three days of fighting Operation *Ring* had failed to achieve its initial objectives and German units were continuing to inflict heavy losses.

Rokossovsky continued probing attacks on 13 January, but his forces were not yet ready to attack the Rossosh River line. Chistiakov's 21st Army captured the abandoned village of Karpovka, but much of XIV.Panzer-Korps slipped away, minus its heavy equipment. The next day, Batov's 65th Army mounted an attack against the centre of the Rossosh line, at Baburkin, but without artillery support – and was repulsed by the remnants of 44.Infanterie-Division. Rokossovsky decided to play it safe and wait until he brought up fresh troops and artillery, so he could mount a proper set-piece attack the next day. However, the Germans knew that all their divisions on the western front were in awful condition and that the Rossosh line would not pose a serious obstacle, so they began pulling back on the night of 14/15 January. By the time that Rokossovsky began his assault on the morning of 15 January, most of the German troops had withdrawn towards Stalingrad, leaving only a few rearguards to delay pursuit. In the south, the 57th and 64th armies finally captured the village of Elkhi and forced VIII.Armee-Korps to pull back, as well. On 16 January, the 51st Guards Rifle Division from the 21st Army pushed forwards and captured Pitomnik airfield, which reduced the rapidly dwindling airlift to just Gumrak airfield. By this point, the Luftwaffe was

Heeresgruppe Don situation, January–February 1943

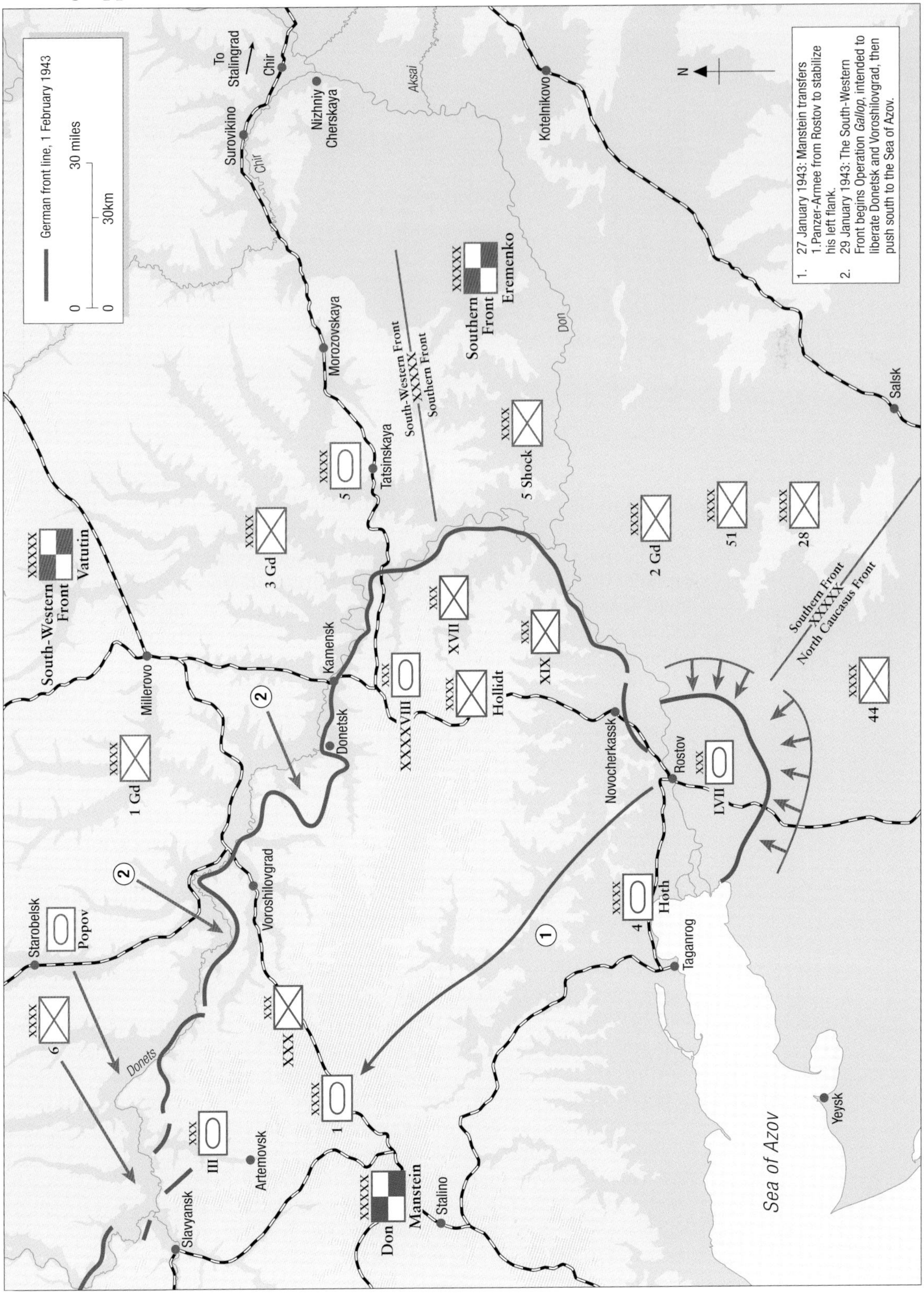

German front line, 1 February 1943

0   30km

0   30 miles

N

1. 27 January 1943: Manstein transfers
    1.Panzer-Armee from Rostov to stabilize
    his left flank.
2. 29 January 1943: The South-Western
    Front begins Operation *Gallop*, intended to
    liberate Donetsk and Voroshilovgrad, then
    push south to the Sea of Azov.

To
Stalingrad

Chir

Surovikino

Nizhniy
Cherskaya

Chir

Aksai

Kotelnikovo

Morozovskaya

Don

Salsk

XXXXX
Southern
Front   Eremenko

South-Western Front
XXXXX
Southern Front

Tatsinskaya

XXXX
5

XXXX
5 Shock

XXXX
3 Gd

XXXXX
South-Western
Front   Vatutin

Kamensk

XXX
XVII

XXX
XIX

XXXX
2 Gd

XXXX
51

XXXX
28

XXX
XXXXVIII

XXXX
Hollidt

Southern Front
XXXXX
North Caucasus Front

Millerovo

Donetsk

②

XXXX
1 Gd

Novocherkassk

Rostov

XXX
LVII

XXXX
44

Starobelsk

②

Voroshilovgrad

XXXX
Hoth
4

Hoth

XXXX
Popov

XXX
XXX

①

Taganrog

XXXX
6

Donets

XXXX
1

Sea of Azov

Yeysk

XXX
III

Artemovsk

XXXXX
Don
Manstein   Stalino

Slavyansk

77

delivering fewer than 100 tons of supplies per day and 6.Armee's logistics system was near collapse. The loss of Pitomnik also forced the Luftwaffe to withdraw its fighter units, which left transport flights without any protection. On the night of 17/18 January, Rokossovsky decided to pause his offensive in order to replenish his ammunition supplies and reorganize his units for the final series of attacks. The Don Front had suffered about 26,000 casualties in one week of fighting and had lost half its armour. Voronov developed and submitted a modified plan to Stalin, who agreed to a brief pause.

The Germans used the respite to try to organize a final defence, as well as to evacuate key personnel. Hitler ordered Hube and some of his veteran panzer officers, such as Oberst Hyazinth Graf Strachwitz, Oberstleutnant Willy Langkeit and Hauptmann Haen, to fly out of the pocket. In addition, General der Pioniere Erwin Jaenecke, commander of IV.Armee-Korps, and six division commanders (including one Romanian) were flown out. Altogether, during the 70 days of the airlift, VIII.Fliegerkorps managed to evacuate 24,760 wounded and 5,150 key personnel from the Stalingrad pocket. Over 12,000 wounded remained in the pocket, with negligible medical treatment. The 6.Armee's final defensive line lay just west of the city, with Gumrak airfield just behind.

Rokossovsky resumed his offensive on 21 January, with Batov's 65th Army launching another attack that crushed the remaining combat value out of the German 44.Infanterie-Division and 76.Infanterie-Division. At the same time, the 24th and 66th armies hit XI.Armee-Korps hard in the north-east sector of the pocket. The next morning, the Don Front launched a powerful set-piece offensive, which struck all around 6.Armee's perimeter. Once again, Soviet artillery was heavily concentrated and Rokossovsky now had two artillery divisions in support (1st and 11th). German artillery was silent, for lack of ammunition. Batov's 65th Army blasted a wide gap in the VIII.Armee-Korps front, which could not be closed. Threatened by the enemy advance. Paulus evacuated his headquarters from Gumrak and relocated to the Univermag (TsUM) Department Store in southern Stalingrad. Soviet attacks continued on 23 January, with the 21st Army overrunning

Soviet T-34 tanks and infantry assemble near the Krasny Oktyabr Steel Plant in Stalingrad, late January 1943. Due to heavy losses of infantry and tanks, Rokossovsky slowed down the operations tempo during the final week of Operation *Ring*. Once the steel plant was retaken, Chuikov's forces pushed west to link up with the approaching 21st Army near Mamaev Kurgan. (Süddeutsche Zeitung, Bild 02884715)

Gumrak airfield. Remnants of the Romanian 20th Infantry Division and 1st Cavalry Division fought near Gumrak, and were praised by the Germans for their steadfastness. Before Gumrak was lost, the Germans created a small airstrip atop the Mamaev Kurgan, dubbed 'Stalingradskaya', but it was only operational for two days. The last German flight out of the Stalingrad pocket occurred at 1045hrs on 23 January. Thereafter, 6.Armee could only be supplied via parachute by aerial supply canisters. The German IV.Armee-Korps was also pushed back 4km into the southern part of the city.

Heavy fighting continued on the western and southern outskirts of the city on 24–25 January, but the exhausted German troops were steadily pushed back. The last few tanks were now immobilized for lack of fuel. Paulus requested that 6.Armee be allowed to surrender, but Hitler refused. Rokossovsky launched another major offensive pulse on the morning of 26 January, with Chistiakov's 21st Army smashing through broken German units to link up with Chuikov's 62nd Army, thereby slicing the Stalingrad pocket into two pieces. Strecker's XI.Armee-Korps held the northern pocket, while most of the rest of the remnants of 6.Armee, including Paulus, were in the southern pocket. The first major German unit, about 1,800 troops from 297.Infanterie-Division, surrendered. Generalmajor Alexander von Hartmann, commander of 71.Infanterie-Division, decided to die in action and was shot dead while firing at the enemy with a rifle. Now that the Stalingrad pocket was drastically reduced in size, Stavka began withdrawing formations in order to refit them and redeploy them to other sectors. Galinin's 24th Army was withdrawn into reserve on 27 January, followed by the 57th Army on 29 January. Due to heavy losses, the Don Front was running short on infantry in the final battles and Rokossovsky deliberately adopted a more methodical approach in order to keep his casualties down.

Without food or ammunition, the end came rapidly for 6.Armee. Units were all jumbled up and most troops in the front lines had not eaten for several days. Rokossovsky assigned the 21st, 57th and 64th armies to reduce the southern pocket, while the 62nd, 65th and 66th armies reduced the northern pocket. A major attack by the 21st and 62nd armies on

RETREAT INTO STALINGRAD, 2100HRS, 22 JANUARY 1943 (PP. 80–81)

By the twelfth day of Operation *Ring*, the battered 6.Armee could no longer maintain a continuous front line. All divisions were reduced to mixed battlegroups with troops from many different formations, including support units and Luftwaffe personnel. Ammunition and fuel were exhausted and the troops' will to fight was sapped by cold and starvation. Discipline was also near collapse in some units.

On the night of 22/23 January 1943, the remnants of the shattered IV.Armee-Korps, VIII.Armee-Korps and XIV.Panzer-Korps abandoned the last defensive positions west of Stalingrad and began pulling back into the outskirts of the ruined city. Nor was there any succour to be found in the wreckage of Stalingrad, where German troops from LI.Armee-Korps were surviving each day on one slice of bread and soup made from horsemeat and melted snow. Pitomnik airfield had already been lost and Gumrak airfield was already under attack, meaning that the army's logistic situation was near breakdown.

In this scene, survivors from XIV.Panzer-Korps (**1**) march towards the ruins of Stalingrad, past a battlefield littered with abandoned German equipment. The Marder III tank destroyers (**2**) had played a vital role in the defence of the Stalingrad perimeter, inflicting great losses on attacking Soviet tanks, but were now immobilized for lack of fuel. Likewise, the German division and corps artillery units, equipped with weapons like this 15cm sFH18 howitzer (**3**), had been a bulwark of the defence until they fell silent for lack of shells. Even 6.Armee's large fleet of over 10,000 motor vehicles were now immobilized and all its horses eaten, limiting the remaining troops to movement by foot. The German troops themselves are a sorry lot, dirty and lice-ridden, suffering from malnourishment and frostbite. The soldiers shuffle along, with the greatest effort and the weaker ones fall out, left behind to freeze to death in the snow. Defeat is staring them in the face and they recognize it. It is only through the efforts of a few hardened veterans and dedicated junior officers that units are able to maintain any kind of cohesion, but 6.Armee is rapidly disintegrating into an armed mob.

The TsUM Department Store, or Univermag, in central Stalingrad, which was Paulus' last headquarters. Paulus remained in the basement for most of the last two weeks of the battle and lost interest in the conduct of the battle and the welfare of his men. Despite his criticism of Paulus' conduct, Hitler would repeat this behaviour two years later, in his own underground bunker in Berlin. (Author's collection)

30 January caused a partial collapse in the southern pocket, and Seydlitz was captured. From the prisoners, the Soviets were able to learn the location of Paulus' headquarters, and Shumilov's 64th Army assigned the 38th Separate Motorized Rifle Brigade to capture the TsUM department store. Informed that Stalingrad was about to fall, Hitler decided to promote Paulus to Generalfeldmarschall via radio, in the hope that Paulus would choose suicide instead of surrender. Instead, Paulus accepted the promotion and chose to ignore the implicit suggestion. Soldiers from the 38th Motorized Brigade approached the TsUM department store on the morning of 31 January and demanded that the occupants surrender. At 0715hrs, Paulus and his staff surrendered, followed soon thereafter by the rest of IV.Armee-Korps.

A Soviet soldier, looking towards the TsUM Department Store, waves a red flag to celebrate the surrender of 6.Armee. After six months of heavy combat, the Stalingrad campaign ended with an unusual silence falling over the ruins of the wrecked city. (Author's collection)

SOVIET

A. 62nd Army
B. 64th Army (initial positions)
C. 57th Army (initial positions)
D. 21st Army (initial positions)
E. 65th Army (initial positions)
F. 24th Army (initial positions)
G. 66th Army (initial positions)
H. 64th (final positions)
I. 57th Army (final positions)
J. 21st Army (final positions)
K. 65th Army (final positions)
L. 66th Army (final positions)

64 XXXX — **SHUMILOV**

66 XXXX — **ZHADOV**

57 XXXX — **TOLBUKHIN**

24 XXXX — **GALANIN**

65 XXXX — **BATOV**

21 XXXX — **CHISTIAKOV**

24TH ARMY

65TH ARMY

65TH ARMY
21ST ARMY

GONCHARA

PITOMNIK

21ST ARMY

57TH ARMY

VOROPONOVO STATION

57TH ARMY

PESCHANKA

64TH ARMY

EVENTS

21 January 1943
1. 1005hrs: Batov's 65th Army attacks the left flank of the 76.Infanterie-Division near Hill 120 with four rifle divisions and tanks, advancing 2.5km.

2. 1005hrs: Chistiakov's 21st Army attacks with four rifle divisions and overruns the 44.Infanterie-Division positions around Gonchara.

3. Evening: The 60.Infanterie-Division evacuates Kuzmichi and falls back to a new line near Drevniy Val, while the 113.Infanterie-Division pulls back to Konnyi station.

22 January
4. 1000hrs: Batov's 65th Army continues to push back the VIII.Armee-Korps remnants and gets within 2km of Gumrak. Paulus evacuates his headquarters.

5. Two rifle divisions from the 24th Army and one from the 65th Army capture the Novaya Nadezhda state farm.

6. Tolbukhin's 57th Army captures Voroponovo station and Alekseevka.

23 January
7. Shumilov's 64th Army attacks with four rifle divisions, capturing Peschanka and forcing the IV.Armee-Korps back 4km.

8. The 24th Army captures Konnyi station and Drevniy Val, forcing the 113.Infanterie-Division to retreat towards Gorodishche.

9. The last German flight out of the Stalingrad pocket occurrs at 1045hrs on 23 January from Stalingradskaya.

24 January
10. The 21st Army finally captures Gumrak airfield after heavy fighting.

11. The 64th Army advances into the Minina suburb of southern Stalingrad.

25 January
12. The 65th Army captures Gorodishche and Aleksandrovka.

13. The 21st Army advances towards the Mamaev Kurgan.

14. The German XI.Armee-Korps evacuates Orlovka and pulls back towards the STZ.

26 January
13. 1100hrs: Chistiakov's 21st Army smashes through the broken remnants of VIII.Armee-Korps with two Guards Rifle divisions and 25 KV-1 tanks and links up with Chuikov's 62nd Army, thereby slicing the Stalingrad pocket into two pieces.

14. The 57th and 64th armies destroy most of the German IV.Armee-Korps and reach the Tsaritsa gully. The first German units begin to surrender.

29 January
15. Powerful attacks by the 21st and 57th armies overrun the XIV.Panzer-Korps in the southern pocket.

31 January
16. 0715hrs: Paulus surrenders and the southern pocket collapses.

1 February
17. 1000hrs: The 65th and 66th armies launch a powerful concentric attack on Strecker's XI.Armee-Korps, which inflicts heavy losses on the defenders.

2 February
18. 1400hrs: With its food and ammunition exhausted, the northern pocket surrenders.

THE FINAL PHASE OF OPERATION *RING*, 21 JANUARY–2 FEBRUARY 1943

After a brief pause to restock ammunition and replace losses, Rokossovsky resumed his offensive against the disintegrating 6.Armee on 21 January. However, this time the Soviets attacked more methodically, trying to limit their own casualties in what both sides recognized would be the final days of the fight for Stalingrad.

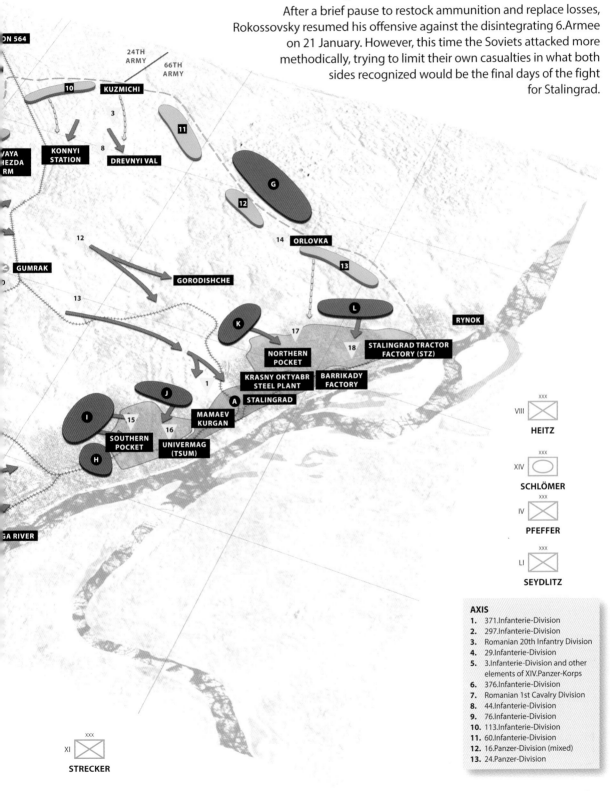

ON 564

24TH ARMY

66TH ARMY

KUZMICHI

10

3

11

8

KONNYI STATION

VAYA HEZDA RM

DREVNYI VAL

G

12

12

14 ORLOVKA

GUMRAK

13

GORODISHCHE

13

L

RYNOK

K

17

18

STALINGRAD TRACTOR FACTORY (STZ)

NORTHERN POCKET

KRASNY OKTYABR STEEL PLANT

BARRIKADY FACTORY

1

J

A STALINGRAD

I

15

MAMAEV KURGAN

SOUTHERN POCKET

16

UNIVERMAG (TSUM)

H

GA RIVER

VIII ⊠ ˣˣˣ
HEITZ

XIV ⬭ ˣˣˣ
SCHLÖMER

IV ⊠ ˣˣˣ
PFEFFER

LI ⊠ ˣˣˣ
SEYDLITZ

AXIS
1. 371.Infanterie-Division
2. 297.Infanterie-Division
3. Romanian 20th Infantry Division
4. 29.Infanterie-Division
5. 3.Infanterie-Division and other elements of XIV.Panzer-Korps
6. 376.Infanterie-Division
7. Romanian 1st Cavalry Division
8. 44.Infanterie-Division
9. 76.Infanterie-Division
10. 113.Infanterie-Division
11. 60.Infanterie-Division
12. 16.Panzer-Division (mixed)
13. 24.Panzer-Division

XI ⊠ ˣˣˣ
STRECKER

Note: gridlines are shown at intervals of 10km (6.2 miles)

Soldiers from 6.Armee walk out of the shattered ruins of Stalingrad into Soviet captivity – the first time in military history that an entire German field army had surrendered. Malnourished and suffering from a myriad of cold weather illnesses, about half the prisoners died within three months. (Author's collection)

Strecker's XI.Armee-Korps, in the ruins of the Stalingrad Tractor Factory, managed to hold out in the northern pocket for another two days. He had about 50,000 troops, the remnants of seven divisions. At 0830hrs on 1 February, the Don Front launched a powerful concentric attack on Strecker's XI.Armee-Korps with the 65th and 66th armies, preceded by a 90-minute artillery barrage. The 16th Air Army also delivered powerful bombing attacks on the encircled German pockets. Although Strecker's XI.Armee-Korps resisted desperately, its western and northern fronts were ripped apart. About 4,000 Germans were killed or wounded in the final assault and over 20,000 captured. Strecker still wanted to resist, but his subordinates took matters into their own hands and initiated talks with the Soviets. By the morning of 2 February, the troops in the northern pocket were virtually out of ammunition and Strecker finally agreed to surrender at around 0700hrs. At 0920hrs, Heeresgruppe Don received its last message from Stalingrad, indicating that resistance was ending.

Although the main event was over, at least 5,000–10,000 German soldiers and Hiwis remained at large in and around Stalingrad for two weeks after the formal surrender. Some small groups tried to escape through the Soviet ring, while others sought to hide in basements or underground shelters. The NKVD ruthlessly hunted down these evaders, eliminating the last around 15 February. Although the Soviets claimed to have taken 91,000 Axis prisoners at Stalingrad, the actual numbers are unclear and may have been as high as 107,800 (including about 700 Croats and 3,000 Romanians). Given that about 6,000 troops were evacuated from the pocket by air in January, it would appear that roughly 98,000 Axis troops died in the final three weeks of the Battle of Stalingrad. In contrast, Rokossovsky's Don Front suffered about 48,000 casualties in the last three weeks, including 12,000 dead. It should not be forgotten that roughly 80,000 civilians died in and near

General Strecker's XI.Armee-Korps in the northern pocket was the last force to surrender on 2 February. Note that these prisoners are actually marching in formation and some are still wearing helmets – a testament to the higher sense of discipline and morale in Strecker's corps. Also note the odd presence of two Russian children at the front of the column. (Author's collection)

Stalingrad during the campaign, leaving only a pitiful handful in the wrecked city by mid-February 1943.

Except for Paulus and a few senior officers, 6.Armee's prisoners were marched to the village of Krasnoarmeisk, 14km south-east of Beketovka, where the NKVD had set up a temporary PoW cage. Most of the prisoners were in poor physical condition due to malnutrition, wounds and cold-weather injuries, which led to thousands of deaths within a matter of weeks. Eventually, many of the survivors were sent to Beketovka Camp 108, where

The NKVD spent two weeks after the battle ended ruthlessly hunting down German soldiers trying to hide in the ruins of Stalingrad. Former Hiwis also attempted to avoid capture, since they risked NKVD field tribunals for treason. (Author's collection)

they would spend the next several years; the men in this camp were used to clear rubble from the Stalingrad battlefield. In March 1943, the NKVD began sending the rest of 6.Armee's enlisted personnel by rail to 14 different PoW camps in the interior of the Soviet Union. For example, 8,007 prisoners were sent to Pokrovsky Camp #127 near Saratov; 1,526 died en route and another 4,663 men died within six weeks of arriving at the camp. Captured German officers were sent to three camps – Oranki #74, Elabuga #97 and Krasnogorsk #27 – where they were interrogated and some were tried with war crimes. The NKVD used a combination of carrot and stick to induce captured senior officers to join an anti-fascist movement, which eventually became the League of German Officers (Bund Deutscher Offiziere, BDO). Seydlitz became the senior collaborator among the captured 6.Armee officers and headed the BDO, which earned him a death sentence in absentia in the Third Reich. Although some crippled prisoners were released in 1947–48, most of the 6.Armee prisoners were not released until after Stalin's death in 1953. Ultimately, only about 6,000 of the prisoners taken at Stalingrad ever returned to Germany.

German prisoners from the southern pocket trudge past the iconic Grain Elevator, which had given them such trouble four months prior. Note the Soviet guard on the right side of the column and the fact that only a single German in this group has a winter camouflage suit. (Süddeutsche Zeitung, 00003918, Foto: Scherl)

ANALYSIS

The Battle of Stalingrad was one of the greatest blood-lettings in modern military history and one of the most decisive moments of World War II. Indeed, there is no doubt that the fate of Hitler's Third Reich was sealed at Stalingrad. The loss of the entire 6.Armee at Stalingrad was an unprecedented catastrophe in Germany military history, although it would be repeated many times over the next two years. Incredibly, the German leadership – through a process of deliberate but ill-judged decision-making – managed to snatch defeat from what had had seemed like the jaws of victory back in September 1942. Over the course of the six-month long Stalingrad campaign, the Wehrmacht suffered in excess of 370,000 casualties, including at least 235,000 dead, missing or captured. Romanian forces suffered over 160,000 casualties and Italian forces another 114,000, which effectively removed two more Axis field armies from the Eastern Front (soon followed by the destruction of the Hungarian Second Army). Twenty-two entire divisions had been destroyed at Stalingrad and some units outside the pocket, such as 22.Panzer-Division, had to be disbanded. The Ostheer had committed some of its best units to the Stalingrad campaign and no fewer than 12 of its 41 *Panzer-Abteilungen* and four of its 22 *Sturmgeschütz-Abteilungen*, along with about 5,000 of their veteran personnel, were lost. The loss of over 600 tanks, plus large amounts of artillery and motor vehicles, was staggering. Despite great bravery shown by Luftwaffe aircrew, the Stalingrad airlift was a total failure, which rarely supplied more than 10–20 per cent of 6.Armee's logistical requirements and cost VIII.Fliegerkorps a total of 488 aircraft (including one-third of all Ju 52 transports in the Luftwaffe). Defeat at Stalingrad not only cost the Wehrmacht the strategic initiative in Russia, but left the Ostheer in an impoverished state in terms of personnel and materiel, which it was never able to rectify.

Hitler's obstinate decision to continue trying to grind forward at Stalingrad and occupy every last square metre of urban ruins in October–November 1942, rather than accept that Stalingrad's armament industries had been destroyed and pull 6.Armee back to the Don bridgeheads, was the proximate cause of the disaster. While Hitler did eventually recognize the threat to 6.Armee's flanks and ordered counter-measures, he failed to ensure that adequate mobile reserves and defensive plans were put in place. Both von Weichs and Paulus share considerable blame for not deploying more forces behind the Romanians and fortifying key points such as Kalach. The protracted defence of Millerovo demonstrates how well-fortified positions could fend off Soviet armour. Likewise, Hube's XIV.Panzer-Korps, if better

deployed, might have made it much more difficult for the Red Army to close its jaws around 6.Armee. Once 6.Armee was encircled, an immediate breakout was the only chance to save even a portion of the army, but Hitler and Paulus ensured that this brief window of opportunity was wasted. Both the Luftwaffe airlift and *Wintergewitter* were forlorn hopes with little chance of success; indeed both efforts were conducted in a messy, inefficient style that was very uncharacteristic of the Wehrmacht. Von Manstein and a coterie of other local German field commanders did pull off a near-miracle in preventing the complete collapse of the southern front and saving Heeresgruppe A in the Caucasus, but as Churchill quipped in 1940, wars are not won by retreats.

Four days after 6.Armee surrendered, Hitler told von Manstein, 'I alone bear the responsibility for Stalingrad.' In strategic terms, Hitler used the catastrophe to harness Germany's industry and people for total war. Armaments production increased dramatically in 1943 and the Wehrmacht was able to raise new divisions to replace the ones lost at Stalingrad. Although the German population was rattled by the defeat and covert resistance in the officer corps became more active, Hitler managed to convince most of his people that the *Endseig* (final victory) could still be achieved with further large helpings of unconditional sacrifice. With defeat now a real possibility – and the fear of being brought to account for crimes committed in the name of the Third Reich – German civilian and military resistance became increasingly fanatical.

The Ostheer did learn some valuable lessons from the Stalingrad debacle. When other German forces were encircled later in the war, commanders knew that they must conduct a breakout as soon as possible, whether Hitler

Abandoned German tanks after the Battle of Stalingrad. The 6.Armee lost nearly 300 tanks in the pocket, as well as about 35 assault guns and 30 Marder III tank destroyers. Due to fuel shortages and lack of spare parts, 6.Armee was only able to keep a fraction of its armour operational in the final weeks of the battle. Note that all the tanks here have had their tracks removed and even roadwheels, suggesting cannibalization efforts to keep a few tanks going to the end. (Author's collection)

General der Artillerie Walter von Seydlitz-Kurzbach, commander of LI.Armee-Korps. Although a highly decorated hero of the Third Reich and scion of a well-known Prussian family, Seydlitz openly collaborated with the NKVD in Soviet captivity and formed the anti-Nazi League of German Officers (Bund Deutscher Offiziere – BDO). Seydlitz's actions earned himself a death sentence in absentia from the Third Reich and the contempt of most of his fellow captured officers. The Soviets rewarded his collaboration with their own death sentence passed on him – which was later commuted. (Courtesy of the Central Museum of the Armed Forces, Moscow via Stavka)

authorized it or not. Consequently, in the Battle of the Korsun Pocket (February 1944) the Germans were able to save two-thirds of the encircled force. Hube, given command of 1.Panzer-Armee, had his entire army surrounded in March 1944, but led a successful breakout that saved not only his 200,000 troops but even a good deal of their equipment. After Stalingrad, German commanders also got much better at organizing ad hoc relief operations, which encouraged isolated units to resist instead of surrender. In operational terms, defeat at Stalingrad caused Hitler to re-evaluate the German position in the East, which led him to authorize withdrawals from the Demyansk and Rzhev salients – thereby freeing up many divisions for use elsewhere. Stalingrad taught the OKH and commanders like von Manstein the necessity of creating a strong, mobile reserve to deal with unexpected crises, but Hitler would not endorse this recommendation because it implied shifting to the defence. Instead, as soon as the Wehrmacht partially recovered from Stalingrad, Hitler began planning for new offensives in the East.

Stalingrad was a triumph for the Red Army, although the cost had been immense. Between late July 1942 and the surrender of 6.Armee, Soviet forces in the Stalingrad sector had suffered 1,129,619 casualties, including 478,741 dead or missing. In other words, in this one campaign the Red Army suffered more losses than either the United Kingdom or the United States suffered in the entire duration of World War II – a point that Russian historians continue to emphasize. In addition to heavy personnel casualties, the Red Army also lost 4,341 tanks, a great deal of artillery and 2,769 aircraft in the Stalingrad campaign. Although victory at Stalingrad left the Red Army in a stronger position than the Ostheer, it would not be until mid-1943 that Soviet industry could provide it with enough materiel to achieve an overwhelming advantage. The Red Army won at Stalingrad because it had learned from its previous mistakes. In the three offensive operations conducted against Heeresgruppe B/Don between November 1942 and January 1943, Red Army commanders demonstrated an increased ability to mass combat power in critical sectors in order to achieve a breakthrough. The Soviet use of massed artillery to smash enemy positions and the use of airpower to interdict the German airlift were also major improvements over past performance. Yet the main game-changer from the Soviet perspective was that Stalin and his political commissars accepted the need for greater operational flexibility and less micro-management, which enabled Red Army commanders to fight battles in a more professional manner. At the soldier-level, the Axis defeat at Stalingrad created a huge morale boost for the Red Army and its personnel now recognized that they were on the path towards eventual victory.

Nevertheless, the Red Army's offensives in late 1942 and early 1943 did not run smoothly, due to unexpected enemy resistance and lacklustre intelligence and logistic support. Soviet military planners still approached warfare with a mathematical mindset, assuming that with enough artillery bombardment, and enough infantry and tanks, enemy resistance would simply collapse. Yet this mindset ignored the moral dimension of combat, which became increasingly salient in the final stages of the Battle of Stalingrad. The trapped soldiers of 6.Armee fought tenaciously because they did not expect to survive captivity – which turned out to be true for most of them. Indeed, the trapped 6.Armee fought longer and harder than other German formations surrounded by the Anglo-American forces in 1944–45 precisely because they knew they were in a no-quarter environment. In contrast, three months after Stalingrad, Panzer-Armee Afrika walked into Allied PoW cages in Tunisia after offering far less fanatical resistance. Soviet operational-level intelligence significantly underestimated the number of troops in Stalingrad and failed to properly assess enemy mobile reserves, which undermined the Red Army's ability to achieve its objectives in a timely manner. The fact that forward Soviet armoured units had to ask a local peasant about the status and location of

the critical bridge at Kalach indicates that the intelligence process was not providing effective support to combat units. Furthermore, the inability of Soviet logistic units to efficiently push fuel and ammunition forward to fast-moving mechanized units often led to a start–stop manoeuvre tempo. These twin weaknesses – intelligence and logistics – would contribute to the failure of Operation *Star* in March 1943, which allowed the Germans to temporarily regain the initiative. Nevertheless, the Red Army would gradually improve both its intelligence and logistical capabilities, even though it was still struggling to climb a steep learning curve during the Stalingrad campaign.

Another major lesson for the Red Army, learned at great cost at Stalingrad, was that offensives needed to have multiple echelons in order to overwhelm strong enemy defences. By conducting *Uranus* with a single echelon, Soviet commanders lacked adequate follow-on forces to reinforce success and were forced to constantly transfer units between armies. The Germans were adept at dealing with single-echelon offensives, which they had demonstrated repeatedly at Kotluban in September–October 1942. However, the German tendency to operate within thin resource margins left them ill suited to handle enemy offensives that were conducted with more than a single echelon. Once resources permitted, the Red Army would switch to multi-echelon offensives in the summer of 1943, which enabled them to relentlessly pound German defences until they broke. Thus, the Stalingrad campaign not only deprived the Wehrmacht of its last opportunity to achieve a major success in Russia, but it provided the Red Army with the moral and professional tools to turn the tide and begin on the path towards eventual victory in Berlin.

Hitler ordered a heroic monument to be created in the Zeughaus in Berlin, honouring the sacrifice of 6.Armee at Stalingrad. When Hitler went to the Zeughaus on 21 March 1943 to view the sculpture and commemorate Heroes Memorial Day (*Heldengedenktag*), Oberst Rudolf von Gersdorff attempted to assassinate him with a concealed explosive device. However, Hitler left the exhibit after a brief visit and Gersdorff disarmed the bomb without being detected. (Süddeutsche Zeitung, Bild 00021911, Foto: Scherl)

THE BATTLEFIELD TODAY

In the previous two volumes in this trilogy, I discussed modern battlefield memorials related to the German advance to Stalingrad and the fighting in the city itself. In this volume, I will discuss sites related to Operation *Uranus* and the final surrender of 6.Armee. The most significant memorial for this period of the campaign is the 'Union of the Fronts' monument near Kalach. The centrepiece of the memorial is a 25m-high cluster of statues of Soviet tankers and motorized infantrymen shaking hands, symbolizing the link up of the South-Western and Stalingrad fronts on 23 November 1942. Although gigantic in proportions, the monument offers little in terms of historical value. Nearby, Kalach – which was designated a 'hero city' – has a considerable number of military monuments and memorials, with one listing the names of over 3,000 residents who died during the war. However, the Russians have a tendency to mix equipment from different periods and even different wars in the same venue. Near a T-70 light tank in a park in Kalach, there is a memorial to Russian soldiers lost in more recent conflicts, including Afghanistan, Laos, Syria and a number of other places.

The 'Union of the Fronts' monument located in Pyatimorsk, 6km south-east of Kalach, depicts a romanticized version of tankers and infantrymen completing the link up that encircled 6.Armee at Stalingrad. In fact, the link up was poorly coordinated and resulted in a fratricidal shooting incident with casualties on both sides. (Author's collection)

The areas directly involved with the conduct of Operation *Uranus* are now mostly open steppe, with little or nothing to mark the events of 1942. Towns like Kletskaya, Kremenskaya and Serafimovich offer next to nothing for historically minded visitors to see, aside from a few small cemeteries. The situation is much the same south-east of Stalingrad in towns like Abganerovo, and even Lake Sarpa is now little more than a shallow marsh. In Verkhne Kumski, there is a torch-like memorial over a mass grave for Soviet troops who died delaying Hoth's advance.

Some of the airfields involved in the Stalingrad airlift are still in use, but others have simply disappeared into the mist of history. Gumrak airfield is now Volgograd International Airport. A number of old German bunkers are located 2km south-east of the airport and a number of German dead were hastily buried in this area – it is now a prime site for those digging for battlefield artefacts. In contrast, Pitomnik is just a typical stretch of open steppe, bisected by a dirt road and lacking even a basic historical marker. Not far from Pitomnik, there is a monument to Leytenant Aleksei F. Naumov and his crew (91st Tank Brigade), whose KV-1 heavy tank was destroyed in fighting near the airfield on 21 January 1943. Morozovsk airbase is still used by the Russian Air Force and currently hosts a regiment of Su-27 Flankers. Tatsinskaya lies abandoned, but is still recognizable as an airfield.

In the final weeks of the Battle of Stalingrad, Paulus sheltered in the basement of the Univermag (TsUM) department store, which now hosts a museum dedicated to this subject. A number of artefacts are displayed, such as Paulus' uniform and staff car, but the most poignant is one of the pathetic decorated Christmas trees fabricated by some of the German troops. It is a small museum, of limited historical value, although it does convey the gloom and isolation of what life inside this underground shelter must have been like. Although thousands of German soldiers are buried in the Rossoshka cemetery, most of 6.Armee's captured soldiers disappeared without a trace, either dying en route to distant PoW camps or held in fields around Beketovka and Krasnoarmeyskiy. One former NKVD PoW camp, Oranki #74 near Nizhny Novgorod, held both German and Romanian prisoners taken at Stalingrad. The camp itself is gone, but its outline is still visible, and German veterans were allowed to place a marker there for the prisoners who died in captivity.

Soviet medal commemorating the defence of Stalingrad. The reverse side inscription reads, 'For our Soviet motherland'. The victory at Stalingrad, although costly, proved to be a great morale booster for both the Red Army and the war-ravaged Soviet people. (Author's collection)

The grave of a fallen Soviet soldier from the 35th Guards Rifle Division near modern Volgograd, neatly topped by a punctured helmet. The Red Army lost over 400,000 soldiers in the six-month Stalingrad campaign, more than double the number the French Army lost at Verdun in 1916. (Author's collection)

FURTHER READING

Primary Sources
Gefechts Bericht, Kampfgruppe Simon, 12 December 1942

Secondary Sources
Bergström, Christer, *Stalingrad: The Air Battle 1942 through January 1943* (Hersham: Ian Allan Publishing, 2007)

Chuikov, Vasily I., *The Battle for Stalingrad* (New York: Holt, Reinhart and Winston, 1964)

Falk, Dann, *The 64th Army at Stalingrad 1942–43* (Falken Books, 2019)

Glantz, David M., *Endgame at Stalingrad, Book 1: November 1942* (Lawrence, KS: University Press of Kansas, 2014)

Glantz, David M., *Endgame at Stalingrad, Book 2: December 1942 – February 1943* (Lawrence, KS: University Press of Kansas, 2014)

Glantz, David M., *From the Don to the Dnepr: Soviet Offensive Operations, December 1942 – August 1943* (London: Frank Cass Publishers, 1991)

Görlitz, Walter, *Paulus and Stalingrad: A Life of Field-Marshal Friedrich Paulus* (New York: Citadel Press, 1964)

Hayward, Joel S. A., *Stopped at Stalingrad: The Luftwaffe and Hitler's Defeat in the East 1942–43* (Lawrence, KS: University Press of Kansas, 1998)

Hill, Alexander, *The Red Army and the Second World War* (Cambridge: Cambridge University Press, 2017)

Holl, Adelbert, *An Infantryman in Stalingrad: From 24 September 1942 to 2 February 1943* (Sydney: Leaping Horsemen Books, 2005)

Jukes, Geoffrey, *Hitler's Stalingrad Decisions* (Berkeley: University of California Press, 1985)

Mark, Jason D., *Death of the Leaping Horseman: The 24th Panzer Division in Stalingrad* (Mechanicsburg: Stackpole Books, 2014)

Mark, Jason D., *Panzerkrieg, Volume 1: German Armoured Operations at Stalingrad* (Sydney: Leaping Horsemen Books, 2017)

Rokossovsky, Konstantin, *Soldatskiy Dolg [A Soldier's Duty]* (Moscow: Military Publishing, 1988)

Scianna, Bastian Matteo, *The Italian War on the Eastern Front, 1941–1943: Operations, Myths and Memories* (Switzerland: Palgrave Macmillan, 2019)

Vasil'ev, H. I., *Tatsinskii Reid [The Tatsinskaya Raid]* (Moscow: Voenizdat, 1969)

A grim reminder of the human cost of the Battle of Stalingrad – the remains of wartime casualties continue to be discovered in the soil around Volgograd in large numbers. There are no heroic flags or banners here, just endless rows of skeletons of those who died in one of the largest and costliest battles in human history. (Author's collection)

INDEX

Page numbers in **bold** refer to an illustration; page numbers in brackets are captions to the illustration.

Abganerovo 34, 39, 58, 93
Aksai River 42, 46 57, 58, 59, 60

Badanov, General-major Vasily M 64, 65, 67
Balck, General-major Hermann 46, 54–55, 67
Batov, General-leytenant Pavel I. 28, 31, 40, 44, 67, 68, 75, 78
Beketovka 5, 25, 34, 87
Borisov, General-major Mikhail D. 28, 30–31, 35, 41, 51
Butkov, General-major Vasily V. 28, 29, 30, 35, 41, 47, 51, 54, 55

Chir River 35, 41, 45, 46, 47
Chir River, Battle of 51, 52 (map), 53–55
Chistiakov, General-major Ivan M. 27, 28, 29, 31, 35, 47, 67, 68, 75, 76, 79
Chiukov, General-leytenant Vasily I. 4, 67, 79

Demyansk 7, 43, 44, 90
Don Front 8, 13, 20, 21, 22, 27, 30, 31, **44** (44), 47, 53, 67, 68, 71–72, 74, 78, 79, 86
Don River 11, 30, 38, 44
Donnerschlag Plan 60
Dumitrescu, General Petre **11** (11), 11, 24, 28, 30, 46

Eremenko, General-polkovnik Andrei I. 8–9, **9** (9), 20, **21**, (21), 21, 22, 30, 31, 41, 53, 57, 58, 59, 60, 67, 70, 71

Filippov, podpolnikov Georgy N. 38–40
Fretter-Pico, Generalleutnant Maximilian 65

Galanin, Lieutenant-General Ivan 40, 44, 67, 75, 79
Gariboldi, General Italo 63
Gehlen, Oberst Reinhard 24, 34
German Air Force 16–17
    VIII.Fliegerkorps 16, 17, 29, 35, 46, 51, 53, 58, 65, 68, 69, 74, 78, 88
    Luftwaffe 4, 16–17, 20, 29, 43–44, **47** (47), 57, 58 68–69, 74, 76, 78, 88
    Luftwaffen-Feld-Divisionen 54
German Army 15–16
    casualties 68, 69, 86–87, 88
    Armee-Abteiling Fretter-Pico 65
    Armee-Abteilung Hollidt 51, 60, 61, 64
    Fremde Heere Ost (FHO) 24, 34
    Führer-Begleit-Bataillon (FBB) 64–65
    Gruppe Spang 65
    Heeresgruppe A 4, 11, 46, 61, 89
    Heeresgruppe B 4, 5, 11, 14, 16, 17, 21, 23, 24, 27, 34, 46, 59, 63, 64
    Heeresgruppe Don 34, 45, 46, 55, 65, 77(map), 86
    Heeresgruppe Mitte 10, 21, 24, 46
    Kampfgruppe 30, 34
    Kampfgruppe Dornemann 35
    Kampfgruppe Hünnersdorff 58, 59
    Kampfgruppe Illig 58
    Kampfgruppe Korntner 53
    Kampfgruppe Keysing 65

Kampfgruppe Oppeln 29, 30
Kampfgruppe Reinbrecht 75
Kampfgruppe Tschücke 46, 51
Kampfgruppe von Hanstein 41–42
Oberkommando der Luftwaffe (OKL) 43–44
Oberkommando des Heeres (OKH) 10, 14, 23, 24, 25, 90
Oberkommando der Wehrmacht (OKW) 43
Ostheer 4, 23–24, 88, 89
II.Armee-Korps 43
IV.Armee-Korps 15, 34, 35, 41, 42, 44, 75, 76, 79, 83
VIII.Armee-Korps 67, 68, 75
XI.Armee-Korps 16, 25, 28, 30, 31, 35, 40, 44, 53, 78, 79, **86** (86), 86
XVII.Armee-Korps 45, 63, 64, 65
LI.Armee-Korps 44, 45, 67
6.Armee 4–5, **5** (5), 10, 14, 15–16, 20, 24, 25, 30, 34, 35, 43–44, 47, 58, 60, 68, 69, 70, 74, 87, 88, 91
    air blockade of **48–50** (50)
    casualties 70, 71
    encirclement of 42, 44, 89
    request to surrender refused by Hitler 79
    retreat by **80–82** (82), **86** (86)
9.Armee 20, 24
3.Infanterie-Division 44, 60, **68** (68), 75, 76
29.Infanterie-Division 25, 34, 35, 39, 42, 60, 75
44.Infanterie-Division 16, 40, 67, 68, 74, 75, 76, 78
76.Infanterie-Division 40, 75, 78
94.Infanterie-Division 44, 70
297.Infanterie-Division 34, 79
298.Infanterie-Division 63, 64
306.Infanterie-Division 46, 65
336.Infanterie-Division 46, 54
376.Infanterie-Division 28, 40, 70
387.Infanterie-Division 63
2.Panzer-Armee 8, 24
4.Panzer-Armee 14, 15, 16, 25
Panzer-Armee Afrika 91
Panzer-Grenadiers 16, 25 34
6.Panzer-Division 24, 46, 57, 59, 60, 65
11.Panzer-Division 46, 54–55, **55** (55), 67
14.Panzer-Division 16, 25, 30, 31, 40, 53, 60, 67
16.Panzer-Division 16, 30, 35, 45, 70
17.Panzer-Division 41, 57, 59
22.Panzer-Division 16, 24, 28, 31, 35, 41, 45, 63, 88
23.Panzer-Division 46, 57, 58
24.Panzer-Division 16, 30, 35, 39, 45
27.Panzer-Division 63, 64
XIV.Panzer-Korps 21, 30, 35, 44, 53, 60, 67, 68, 75, 76, 88–89
LVII.Panzer-Korps 55, 57, 59, 60
XXXXVIII.Panzer-Korps 24, 28, 29, 30, 31, 35, 45, 53, 54, 55, 57
German prisoners of war **86** (86), **87** (87)
Göring, Reichsmarschall Hermann 43, 58
Group Lascar 31, 35, 39, 41
Gumrak airfield 40, 43, 44, 78–79, 93

Haen, Hauptmann Rudolf 75, 78
Heim, Generalleutnant Ferdinand 24, 28, 31, 45
Hitler, Adolf 4, 10, 24, **25** (25), 28 34, 40, 42, 43, 44, 45, 46, 53, 74, 78, 79, 83, 88, 89, 90
Hollidt, General der Infanterie, Karl-Adolf 41, 45, 46, 53–54, 65, 67
horse-drawn transport **13** (13), **47** (47)
Hoth, Generaloberst Hermann **10** (10), 11, 31, 34, 35, 39, 46, 57–58, 59, 63, 68, 70, 71
Hube, General Hans-Valentin 21, 30, 35, 39, 44, 53, 60, 67–68, 70, 75, 76, 78, 88–89, 90

Italy 4, **61** (61)
    casualties 88
    Eighth Army 61, 63, 64
    XXXV Army Corps **64** (64), 64
    Alpini Corps 64
    Cosseria Division 63

Jaenecke, General der Pioniere Erwin 44, 78
Jeschonnek, Generaloberst Hans 42, 43

Kalach 22, 39, 88, 91, 92
Kalach Bridge **36–38** (38), 39–40
Karpovka 41, 42, 53, 76
Kirchner, General der Panzertruppe Friedrich 57, 59
Knobelsdorff, Generalmajor Otto von 54, 55
Korsun Pocket, Battle of 90
Koshary 34, 64
Kotelnikovo 46, 51, 53, 57, 60
Kotluban 5, 20, 21, 91
Krasny Oktyobr Steel Plant **69** (69), **79** (79)
Kravchenko, General-major Andrei G. 29, 31, 35, 40, 42, 47, 67
Krushchev, Nikita 7, **21** (21)
Kuznetsov General-leytenant Vasily I. 61, 63, 64, 65

Lake Sarpa 20, 31, 93
Langkeit, Oberleutnant Willy 70, 78
Lascar, General Mihail 31, 41
League of German Officers 87
Lelyushenko, General Dmitri 45, 61, 63, 64, 65
Leyser, Generalmajor Hans 34, 35, 39, 42

Malinovsky, General-leytenant Rodion I. 58, 59, 60, 63
Manstein, Generalfeldmarschall Erich von 34–35, 43, 45, 46, 51, 57–58, 59, 60, 65, 89, 90
Marinovka salient 41, 47, 67, 68, 70, 71, 75
Millerovo 17, 63, 65, 88
Morozovskaya airfield 43, 46, 54, 63, 64, 68, 93

Naumov, Leytenant Aleksei F. 93

Oblivskaya airfield 46, 51
Operation *Barbarossa* 4, 11
Operation *Blau* 4, 8, 11, 23
Operation *Jupiter* 21, 23

Operation *Little Saturn* 55, 58, **62**, 63–5, 71
Operation *Mars* 21, 23
Operation *Ring* 71, **72–73** (72–73), 74–75, **84–85**
Operation *Saturn* 21, 23, 58, 61, 63
Operation *Star* 91
Operation *Typhoon* 9
Operation *Uranus* 7, 8, 12–13, 16, 17, 21, 22–23, 24, **26** (map), **28** (28), 35, 38, 42, 47, 91, 92–93
Oppeln-Bronikowski, Oberst Hermann von 29, 30
Oranki prisoner-of-war camp 93

Paulus, General der Panzertruppe Friedrich 4, **10** (10), 10–11, 16, 20, 25, 30, 35, 39, 40, 41, 42, 43, 44, 45, 53, 60, 67, 68, 74, 78, 79, 83, 88–89, 93
Pavlov, General-major Petr R. 64, 65
Pitomnik 17, 74, **76** (76) 76, 78, 93
Pliev, General-major Issa Alexandrovich 29, 31, 35, 40, 44, 51, 54
Plodovitoye 34
Pokhlebin, Battle of 57
Popov, General-lytenant Markian M. 55, 59

Rasconescu, Major Gheorghe 45–46
Raus, Generalmajor Erhard 46, 57, 58, 59, 60
Rodin, Colonel General Aleksei 31, 35, 39, 47
Rokossovsky, General-polkovnik Konstantin K. 8 (8), 20, 21, 22, 29, 44, 47, 67, 68, 70, 71, 74, 76, 78, 79
Romanenko, General-leytenant Prokofiy L. 9, 12, 27, 28, 29, 30, 35, 41, 45, 46, 47, 51, 53–54, 61, 63
Romania 4–5, 11, 14–15, **15** (15), 21, 59, 70, 88
    casualties 88
    prisoners of war **39** (39)
    I Corps 64
    IV Corps 31
    V Corps 29, 31
    VI Corps 31, 34, 35, 39, 46, 53, 57, 60
    VII Corps 57, 60
    1st Armoured Division **15**, **16** (16), 24, 28, 29, 31, 35, 41, 45
    Third Army 11, 14, 15, 20, 22, 24, 25, 27, 28, 30, 31, 35, 45–46, 61
    Fourth Army 14, 15, 46
    1st Cavalry Division 31, 40, 80
    7th Cavalry Division 24, 31
    2nd Infantry Division 34
    6th Infantry Division 31, 45
    13th Infantry Division 28, 29
    14th Infantry Division 27, 28
    20th Infantry Division 34, 80
Romanian Air Force 17
Rossoschka cemetery 93
Rostov 4, 11, 23, 61, 63
Rostov-Stalingrad rail line 46
Rotmistrov, General-mayor Pavel A. 55, 58, 59, 60
Rudel, Oberleutnant Hans Ulrich 17, 51
Rzhev salient 20, 21, 24, 90

Schmidt, Generalmajor Arthur 11, 40
Seydlitz-Kurzbach, General der Artillerie Walter von 44, 67, 83, 87, **90** (90)
Shapkin, General-leytenant Timofei T. 39, 42, 57, 58

Shumilov, Colonel General Mikhail 34, 39, 67, 83
Soviet Union
    casualties 4, 68, 86–87, 90
    NKVD 86, **87** (87), 87
    Reserve of the Supreme High Command (RVGK) 12, 14, 22, 55, 74
    Soviet Military Intelligence (GRU) 23
    State Defence Committee (GKO) 7, 13, 20, 22–23
    Stavka 7, 13–14, 20, 21, 22, 23, 42, 47, 53, 55, 61, 67, 68, 70–71
    Air Army (VSS) 14, 27, 51–52, 53, 57, 58, 63
        8th Air Army 69
        16th Air Army 74, 75, 86
    Red Army 4–5, 12–14, 90–91
        South-Western Front 8, 12, 13, 21, 22, 23, 27, 30, 31, 39, 47, 55, 61, 63
        6th Army 63
        21st Army 22, 27–28, 29, 31, 35, 47, 53, 58, 67, 68, 71, 75, 76, 78–79
        24th Army 22, 40, 44, 67, 71, 75, 78, 79
        51st Army 20, 31, 39, 46, 53, 58, 60
        57th Army 20, 34, 39, 41, 42, 53, 60, 67, 70, 75, 76, 79
        62nd Army 4, 22, 67, 79
        64th Army 34, 39, 53, 67, 75, 76, 83
        65th Army 22, 28, 31, 40, 44, 53, 67, 68, 71, 75, 78, 86
        66th Army 22, 44, 53, 70, 78, 86
        4th Cavalry Corps 39, 42, 46, 57, 58
        8th Cavalry Corps 28–29, 30–31, 35, 41, 51
        81st Cavalry Division 57
        1st Guards Army 21, 22, 45, 61, 63, 64
        2nd Guards Army 23, 58, 59, 60, 61, 63
        3rd Guards Army 61, 63, 64, 65
        3rd Guards Cavalry Corps 31, 35, 40, 44–45, 47, 51, 54
        1st Guards Mechanized Corps 61, 64
        2nd Guards Mechanized Corps 60
        3rd Guards Mechanized Corps 60
        14th Guards Rifle Division 27, 63
        15th Guards Rifle Division 42
        39th Guards Rifle Division **75** (75)
        47th Guards Rifle Division 27
        50th Guards Rifle Division 27
        51st Guards Rifle Division 67, 76
        5th Guards Tank Army 28, 29, 30
        8th Guards Tank Brigade 53
        47th Guards Tank Regiment 74
        57th Guards Tank Regiment 75
        36th Mechanized Brigade 42
        4th Mechanized Corps 13, 31, 34, 39, 41, 42, 47, 53, 55, 58, 59
        5th Mechanized Corps 53, **54** (54), 55
        6th Mechanized Corps 60
        9th Mechanized Corps 8
        8th Motorcycle Regiment 46
        119th Rifle Division 27
        126th Rifle Division 58
        169th Rifle Division 34
        302nd Rifle Division 58
        333rd Rifle Division 54
        4th Shock Army 9
        5th Shock Army 55, 59
        3rd Tank Army 9
        5th Tank Army 12, 21, 22, 24, 27, **30** (30), 34, 35, 41, 45, 46, 47, 51, 53, 61

19th Tank Brigade 40
45th Tank Brigade 42
85th Tank Brigade 57
1st Tank Corps 28, 29, 30, 35, 41, 47, 51, 54, 55
4th Tank Corps 29, 31, 35, 40, 42, 47, 67
7th Tank Corps 55, 58–59, 60
13th Tank Corps 34, 39, 42, 53, 58
17th Tank Corps 63, 64
18th Tank Corps 63, 64, 65
23rd Tank Corps 55
24th Tank Corps 64, 65,67
25th Tank Corps 64, 65, 67
26th Tank Corps 28, 31, 35, 39, 47
Sovkhoz, Battle of 54
Stalin, Joseph 4, 21, 58–59, 63, 78, 90
Stalingrad, Battle of 88–91
    chronology of 6
    German monument to **91** (91)
    medals for **93** (93)
    Orders of Battle 17–19
    Soviet monument to **92** (92)
Stalingrad Front 5, 22, 23, 30, **32–33**, 35, 41, 42, 47, 53, 60, 61, 67, 68, 71
Stalingrad Pocket, Battle of **66**, 67–70, 79
Stalingrad Tractor Factory (STZ) 4, 86
Strachwitz, Oberst Hyazinth Graf 78
Strecker, General der Infanterie, Karl 28, 30, 35, 40, 44–45, 79, 86

Tanaschishin, General-major Trofim I. 34, 39, 42, 58
Tatsinskaya airfield 43, 57, 63, 64, 65, 68, 69, 74, 93
Tolbukhin, Marshal Fyodor 34, 39, 41, 42, 67, 70
Trufanov, Colonel General Nikolai 31, 34, 39, 53, 58
Tsaritsyn, Battle of 9
TsUM department store 78, **83** (83), 83, 93

Vasilevskiy, General-polkovnik Aleksandr 7, 21, 47, 53, 61, 63, 71
Vatutin, General-leytenant Nikolai F. **7** (7), 7–8, 21, 22, 39, 47, 51, 54, 55, 61, 63, 64, 65
Verkhe Kumski, Battle of 58–59, 93
Volkov, General Mikhail V. 53, 54, 55
Volskiy, General Vasily 31, 34, 39, 41, 42, 58, 59
Voronov, General-polkovnik Nikolai N. 14, 71, 74–75, 78

weather 69, **74** (74), 74
Weichs, Generaloberst Maximilian von 9–10, 11, 24, 25, 31, 34, 35, 41, 42, 46, 57, 64–65, 88
Winter Counter-Offensive 7, 9, 24
Wintergewitter (*Winter Storm*) 55, **56** (56), 57–61, 68, 70–71, 89
Zeitzler, General der Infanterie, Kurt 25
Zhadov, General Aleksei S. 70
Zhidrov, podpolkovnik, Pyotr K. 42
Zhukov, General Georgy 7, 8, 9, 20, 21, 71